The Labour Market and the Service Sector

THE ECONOMICS
OF THE SERVICE SECTOR
IN CANADA

Series Editors:
Herbert G. Grubel
Michael A. Walker

The Labour Market
and the Service Sector

Klaus Weiermair

THE FRASER
INSTITUTE

This study is part of a general programme of research into the services sector made possible by a contribution from the Department of Regional Industrial Expansion, Government of Canada.

Canadian Cataloguing in Publication Data

Weiermair, Klaus, 1939–

The labour market and the service sector

(The Economics of the service sector in Canada, ISSN 0835-4227)

Bibliography: p.

ISBN 0-088975-142-0

1. Service industries workers –Canada – Supply and demand. 2. Service industries – Canada – Employees. I. Fraser Institute (Vancouver, B.C.). II. Title. III. Series.

HD5718.S452C28 1988   331,12'51'000971   C88-091485-8

61,378

Printed in Singapore.

CONTENTS

Figures and Tables

PREFACE AND SUMMARY

As have many other countries, Canada has seen a major restructuring of her economy over the past 15 years. This change was both caused and facilitated by spectacular growth in service sector industries.

The first chapter of this study provides a brief introduction to the topic. In the second chapter, various hypotheses which describe the pattern of employment in the service economy are reviewed. Recent publications have recognized a multitude of growth determinants in the service economy in addition to the traditional service sector growth explanations of income and price elasticity. Among them the most important have been the differential productivity growth between secondary and tertiary sectors, the division of labour and contracting out, the potential for service sector market expansion, trade and social innovation, and the transformation of final service functions. In terms of service sector development, this suggests that the rise of the service economy has been a far more complex phenomenon than it is usually recognized to be and that one should expect considerable variation of employment growth across different service industries. It also indicates rather substantial and ongoing changes in the underlying job and skill structure of the service economy.

Chapter 3 is an empirical account of employment growth in the Canadian service sector. The analysis is based on a multitude of published and unpublished time series and cross-sectional data. This becomes an indirect test of some of the competing hypotheses set out in the second chapter. The empirical evidence supports the opinion that growth in this sector has been due to a variety of factors and not merely a result of price and income elasticities. The significant variances in growth rates across the different classifications of service sector industries are due to various elements in the changing demand for and nature of service sector jobs. From various analyses of the available data, we note that the period of rapid expansion of the service sector may be coming to an end. Assuming that trends continue, future growth rates will be much lower and will be limited to stagnant personal services and progressively impersonal services. Elements of the changing nature of service sector employment for which there is strong empirical evidence include the rise of part-time work, especially among women and youth, and the large increase in self-employment. Finally, the secular rise of part-time work in service sector industries, the relative shorter job duration in this sector, the greater incidence of multiple job holdings involving service industries and its greater proportion of youth employment indicate high levels of labour market flexibility in these industries. This, in turn, suggests a relative ease in the short-run adjustment and allocation of labour in the service sector.

Chapter 4 examines the changing nature of service sector jobs and the forces responsible for this employment adjustment in terms of changing technologies, occupations and skills. The analysis shows that the evolution of the nature and composition of jobs in the service industries over the past 20 years has, in large part, been dominated by the introduction of information technologies. Firms in the service sector have shown a more rapid adoption of these new technologies than other industries. Other important changes include socio-economic developments which led to the increased feminization of work and an increased emphasis on part-time employment. Deregulation both at home and abroad have led to increased domestic and international competition. It has been argued that these developments caused a higher level of "professionalization" and increases in the span of control for many service sector occupations. In many service operations new technologies have eliminated lower level tasks and have thereby increased both the responsibility and productivity of individual workers. Increases in skill levels have also been observed and can be partly attributed to technological changes. It has been noted that the Canadian education and training system's response to these changes in the service sector may have been both insufficient and slow. As a result, we have noticed increases in the mismatching of jobs and skills expressed in terms of such conventional measures as occupational unemployment and shortage or vacancies.

Chapter 5 takes a closer look at the structure, functioning and performance of labour markets in the Canadian service economy. Here, we observe that until very recently, industrial relations developments have been characterized by a steady increase in the union density of the service sector, pay equity, part-time work and job security, particularly as it relates to the introduction of new technologies, have been the dominant issues in collective bargaining. So far, discussion on the economic rationale, economic effects and ideal legal provisions underlying part-time work and pay equity have engaged many task forces, commissions of inquiry and research reports without however yielding a consensus among researchers or interest groups. The design of effective labour market laws and policies which could address such problems as discrimination or female dominated part-time work has in part been hampered by the complexity of the issues at hand and the multi-varied nature of their determination and variability across different service sector industries. We expect some of these problems to sort themselves out without intervention as we can observe a general trend towards increased flexibility of working time, and as gender related wage and employment differences appear headed towards a long-run decline. Evidence on the industrial relations response to technological change has been equally inconclusive with the exception of its recognized inferiority relative to some foreign experience.

Some interesting and rather positive results have been obtained from tests of the "declining middle" hypothesis. These results suggest that whatever polarization of earnings may have occurred in the Canadian economy over the recent past, have not originated in the service sector. On the contrary, the high mobility and flexibility of labour markets in the service industries have contributed to lower earning differentials in the long-run. Subsequent and limited analyses of wage behaviour have provided the usual and expected results in terms of sex and age related wage differentials as well as well-behaved age-earnings profiles. More surprising has been the observation of small wage effects associated with unionization and the large earning differentials associated with the size of employing establishment. Labour market frictions in the form of unemployment and shortages have worsened over the past 15 years. This has been true for unemployment in the service sector in general but even more so for female service sector unemployment. Most employer surveys which were available at the same time indicated the existence of skill shortages which may imply structural mismatches due to rapid technological change and lagging adjustments in the general system of education and training.

In chapter 6, two case studies developed by the author illustrate some common labour adjustment and industrial relations problems in the service sector.

Finally, chapter 7 summarizes our findings and provides an outlook on expected future manpower issues.

ABOUT THE AUTHOR

Klaus Weiermair is a professor of economics in the Faculty of Administrative Studies at York University in Toronto. He received his M.B.A. and Ph.D. from the Vienna School of Economics and Business Administration. In addition to his teaching at York, Professor Weiermair has been a Visiting Research Fellow at the International Institute of Management in West Berlin and has also taught courses at Ecole Superieure des Sciences Economique et Commerciales (ESSEC), Paris; Nankai University (People's Republic of China); University of Linz (Austria) and Keio University (Tokyo). He has served as an economic consultant for the governments of Ontario, Canada, and Austria as well as for many industrial firms.

Professor Weiermair's areas of expertise and research interests focus on human resources, labour market behaviour, labour adjustment, apprenticeship training, international comparisons, manpower forecasting and planning, youth unemployment, international trade, industrial restructuring, hours of work and overtime, and mandatory retirement. A multilinguist, Professor Weiermair is fluent in French, Italian, German and English and his articles have been published in many North American and European journals. Some of his recent publications include *Promoting Women Entrepreneurship; Industrial Training: Foundation of Japan's Productivity Record; Secular Changes in Youth Labour Markets and Youth Unemployment in Canada; Worker Incentives and Worker Participation: On the Changing Nature of the Employment Relationship; Apprenticeship Training in European Countries: The Lessons for Canada;* and *Objectives and Measures of Co-ordination Between Private and Public Manpower Planning.*

Chapter 1

INTRODUCTION

Originally, the Fraser Institute contracted for research on the labour market behaviour underlying the Canadian service economy. As the study progressed, however, it became apparent that a conceptual understanding of the rise, transformation, and expected further development of the service economy was necessary in order to understand employment and labour adjustment issues.

Chapter 2 provides such a conceptual mapping based on recent theoretical and empirical work in this field (Gershuny and Miles 1983, Petit 1986, and OECD 1986).

In chapter 3, using a multitude of published and unpublished time series and cross-sectional data, the evolution of employment in Canadian service industries is analysed, thereby indirectly testing some of the competing hypotheses discussed in chapter 2.

Chapter 4 provides a further analysis of employment changes in the service economy by examining the changing nature of service sector jobs in terms of changing technologies, occupations and skills. How technological and other changes have intermediated this process of employment adjustment historically will also be investigated.

Chapter 5 takes a closer look at the structure, function and performance of labour markets in the Canadian service economy.

Using two case studies developed by the author, chapter 6 illustrates common labour adjustment and industrial relations problems in the service sector. These case studies examine two business organizations operating in medium and high technology fields.

Finally, chapter 7 provides an outlook on expected future manpower issues.

COMPETING HYPOTHESES OF THE RISE AND PATTERN OF EMPLOYMENT IN THE SERVICE ECONOMY

Questions concerning the employment, utilization, compensation and adjustment of labour in service sector organizations and industries are intrinsically interconnected with the rapid evolution and transformation of output in this sector over the past 20 years. This is not a novel observation. Since labour is a derived factor of production, employment is primarily determined by the level and pattern of final demand.

Because the service sector has expanded suddenly during the post-war period, and because services and service markets are difficult to define, research on service sector growth has lagged (see Gershuny and Miles 1983, and Petit 1986).

Before analysing the employment and labour market behaviour underlying the service economy, an attempt will be made to briefly review the major, and at times competing, hypotheses concerning the structure and behaviour of the service sector in general and specific service sector industries in particular. Instead of providing a lengthy theoretical or empirical discussion concerning the causes and consequences of the service economy, which has filled entire books elsewhere (de Bandt 1985, Petit 1986, Channon 1978, and Gershuny and Miles 1983), this portion of the study will be kept brief.

On Defining Services

Stigler's assertion in 1956 that "no authoritative consensus in either the boundaries or the classification of the service industries exist" (Fuchs 1969, p. 14) appears, unfortunately, to be still valid today. Most authors seek to establish features common to different services and often end up with descriptions rather than defined categories. Furthermore, these descriptions frequently address only the development of different service industries at a given time rather than the enduring characteristics of services per se (D. Thomas 1975). The uncertainty of how to define and subdivide this large set of activities is only superficially overcome by classifying as services those products which appear in four of the International Standard Industries Classification's (ISIC) major divisions: wholesale and retail trades, hotels and restaurants; transport, storage and communications; finance, insurance, real estate and business services; and community, social and personal services.

An alternative and now often used approach is to focus on the consumption characteristic of services. Two different and slightly overlapping classification schemes can be identified. First, Petit (1986, p. 12) distinguishes between the following: (a) business services (accounting, research and development, engineering, advertising, employment agencies); (b) household services (hotels, restaurants, personal care, leisure, repairs); (c) collective services which can be under private or public supervision (health, education, government, defence, non-profit organizations); and (d) integration and intermediation services (trade, transport, communications, insurance and finance).

But Browning-Singlemann (1978) and Gershuny and Miles (1983, p. 14) prefer the following classifications: (a) distribution services (transportation and storage, communication, wholesale trade, retail trade); (b) producer services (banking, credit and other financial services, insurance, real estate, engineering and architectural services, accounting and bookkeeping, legal services, miscellaneous services); (c) social services (medical and health, hospitals, education, welfare and religious services, non-profit organizations, postal services, government, miscellaneous professional and social services); and (d) personal services (domestic services, hotels and lodging places, eating and drinking places, repair services, laundry and dry cleaning, barber and beauty shops, entertainment and recreational services, miscellaneous personal services).

The major differences between the two classification schemes are in how business and intermediation services are categorized. Researchers classified these services differently because they define and analyse contracting out and subcontracting in different ways.

Initially, I will employ the Browning-Singlemann classification. It is a consumption-based approach and offers a somewhat better understanding of the disparate nature of services. Later, when discussing technological change and future trends in service sector employment, reference will be made to the Petit classification because of its emphasis on various aspects of the organization and structure of service production.

Determinants of Growth in the Demand for Services

There is now some agreement that the rise of the service economy cannot be explained solely in terms of growth in final demand, whether demand is calculated using differential elasticities or changing prices and tastes (Fuchs 1982, Gershuny and Miles 1983). Orthodox price and income elasticity measures (which are usually obtained from reduced form equations) probably err because the model has been specified incorrectly. Not surprisingly, empirical results have been inconsistent and disappointing. Gershuny and Miles concluded that "evidence does not appear to support the claim that 'final service products' are intrinsically superior commodities. Instead, the variety of patterns across 6 countries and over time, and across income groups within countries, suggests that what is involved is a process of choice between products in which variegated and changing qualities, including price, compatibility with social and economic infra-structure and convenience, are all assessed" (1983, pp. 32, 35).

The following major structural explanations for the changing level and pattern of the service economy have been reported in the literature:

- differential productivity growth between and within secondary and tertiary sectors;
- division of labour, contracting out, and the role of the manufacturing industry as a leading sector;
- possibilities and limits for market expansion in both the manufacturing and service sectors;
- differential local monopoly character of services due to varying levels of international competition;
- diverging patterns of labour relations developments and "rapport salarial"[1] between secondary and tertiary sectors; and
- social innovation and the transformation of the final service function.

Some of the above explanations are complementary, but others are exclusive.

Differential Productivity Growth, De-Industrialization and Service Sector Growth

Adam Smith's classical idea that increasing returns to scale essentially result from market expansion (in the form of new markets, new products and new methods of production) has been reformulated by many economists who linked market expansion to productivity performance and economic development and growth (Verdoorn 1949, Lewis 1978, and Kaldor 1966). The causal and cumulative sequence below was typically explored in manufacturing, leading to the notion of manufacturing as the "engine" of economic growth (Cornwall 1977).

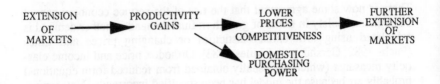

In this context, service sector growth was seen as driven by the same, albeit less easily achievable, factors as manufacturing. Whatever accounts for the differential rise of the international service economy thus appears to hinge on the question of which factors have been at the root of the secular decline in output and productivity growth of the industrial sector. The differential rise of the service economy (e.g., U.S.A. versus Europe or Japan) depends on whether demand or supply is considered central to the secular decline in output and productivity of most industrialized countries (de-industrialization hypothesis).

Economists who see reduced demand as the cause of the slowdown in growth and productivity identify de-industrialization with the inability of the manufacturing sector to overcome the external constraints of balancing trade. This can be seen, for example, in a failure to balance increased imports with a corresponding extension of foreign markets (Singh 1977). Similarly, this school of thought also tends to see only dim prospects for sustained growth in the service economy. Since certain services (e.g., health and education services) cannot be traded extensively in international markets, and since progress in deregulation and trade liberalization is expected to be slow, Petit has concluded that "trade cannot be seen as offering scope for the creation of a new, autonomous external demand capable of helping the old industrialized countries to guarantee the long-term financing of the imports necessary to their growth" (Petit 1986, p. 119).

At the other extreme, supply-side economists interpret causes of de-industrialization as changes in production conditions. They stress a multitude of factors ranging from changes in the price of raw materials (Bruno and Sachs 1982) to investment opportunities (Bailey 1982) to developments in labour relations (Weisskopf, Bowles and Gordon 1983). Their arguments regarding a possible relationship between a stagnating manufacturing base and a growing service sector are, however, much less pronounced and less conclusive. Their arguments depend on alternative assumptions about the labour conditions which underlie changes in production in the service sector. For example, if productivity in the service sector lags behind that in the manufacturing sector (as it did historically in many service industries), and if wage differences between the sectors remain constant in real terms, prices of services must rise in relative terms. Assuming price elasticities behave normally, service demand can be expected to decline eventually. (For a formal treatment, see Skolka 1976.)

Although there are no direct price elasticity effects, similar arguments could be applied to non-marketed services, especially public administration and welfare services. They could also be applied to health and education, where the tax revolts of the late '70s and ensuant public spending restraints suggest that the rising relative price of public service provision is leading to declines in demand. These arguments do not apply to the producer services sector, at least not to that portion which is related to the increased division of labour (contracting out) in the large business manufacturing sector.[2]

Technological change and the potential for substituting capital for labour are clearly mitigating factors in the endogenous process of productivity changes throughout service sector industries. For example, big productivity gains due to technological developments have occurred in telecommunications, services which Baumol describes as "progressive impersonal services" in contrast to "stagnant personal services" which, because of difficulties in product standardization (as is true in patient care or high quality entertainment), defy substitution and other productivity enhancing changes (Baumol 1985 pp. 302-303). By the same token, further expansion of service demand in the future could be viewed optimistically if cost reductions (mainly labour costs) are possible and price elasticities are negative. In this case, the price effect would dominate the income effect, leading to a possible expansion of service output and employment. But, low or falling wages could provide fewer incentives for technological change and, therefore, fewer productivity gains.

Social Innovation and the Transformation of the Final Service Function

In the previous section, relationships between growth in industrial output, sectoral productivity developments and market expansion possibilities, as well as relative wage developments and their relevance for service sector growth were discussed. This section provides a short discussion of the evolution of new technology, work and skills, and the role of social innovation in order to define service provision from a broader perspective of "service functions" within which evolutionary changes can be observed (Gershuny and Miles 1983).

Long-term productivity growth analyses usually show that little conventional innovation has taken place in service industries. But this isn't true if service consumption is viewed in the broader context of service functions which accompany both formal and informal (self-service) modes of service provision. For example, private motoring has replaced final transport services; the domestic washing machine has replaced the purchase of laundering services; and operational home box offices may eventually replace certain entertainment services. According to Gershuny and Miles, these are merely changes towards newer socio-technical systems. New life-styles at work and at home create changes in the modal choices of service provision.

New services tend to take off when the four crucial elements underlying the production function of service provision are changed. These elements include: goods and material equipment (e.g., TV or car); hardware infrastructure (e.g., roads or broadcasting network); software and other intermediate services (e.g., TV programming, maintenance of domestic equipment); and unpaid informal labour.

Based on the recent revolution in information technology, Gershuny and Miles present a long list of projected social innovations in service provision (1983, pp. 126-195). Depicting changes in services in terms of a service provision function not only employs a more dynamic picture of product innovation, but it also highlights the much greater importance of industrial and organizational restructuring which is now taking place within the service economy. Social innovations such as changes in conjugal roles and household production are partly responsible for the changes in the service economy. Consequently, some authors now include the labour force participation rate of women among the determinants of consumer services (Grubel and Walker 1987). While total employment by sector or even within major sectors has remained unchanged, occupational and skill structures may have undergone drastic changes on account of the aforementioned evolution of new technologies and socio-technical systems. Various analyses of changes in work patterns, technology and skill formation in the service sector among OECD countries have reported findings along these lines (OECD/CERI 1986). Future researchers therefore must analyse how major technical and social innovations affect the development and use of human resources in the service sector.

Local Monopoly Character of Services and the Possibilities for Market Expansion and Trade

One of the crucial differences between the production and sale of services as opposed to goods is that services have a high degree of quality and product differentiation because they are often produced jointly between the client and the provider of services. Doctors, lawyers and accountants need both information and co-operation from their clients in order to diagnose an ailment, judge a case or prepare tax returns. The localization of services has been further strengthened by a host of government regulations aimed at securing quality delivery because of information asymmetries between buyer and seller and because of actual or perceived market failures. The outcome has been that many services, particularly the collective services (health, education and public administration), are now being provided by a local monopoly. This trend has far-reaching implications for market expansion potential, tradeability of certain services, and international competition. The underlying input factors are also strongly affected.

Since labour constitutes the major production function input, reference has to be made to the behavioural implications for service sector labour markets. Research on a monopoly's effect on the labour market suggests the following points. First, monopolists are less concerned with cost mini-. mization and profit maximization resulting in organizational slack (Leibenstein 1966). Slack can come in the form of paying wages above marginal product, employing an excessive labour force (over-staffing) or deploying an unwarranted mix of qualifications or skills (e.g., excessive layers of management, over-consumption of certain qualifications, educational gold plating, and excessive specialization). Secondly, these tendencies are likely to be strengthened in the case of unionization since unions are able to drive a harder bargain in product monopoly situations because of low input factor price elasticities (Lewis 1963). And finally, all other things being held constant, prospects for change in industrial relations and labour markets will be small since regulated service providers, their workers, and worker representations are likely to show little economic interest in changing the status quo. Only when a combination of severe government spending cutbacks, deregulation, increased competition, and increased trade of close substitutes emerges will there be sufficient pressure for changes to occur in the underlying market for skills and labour.

On the other hand, deregulation may be difficult to achieve if there is no general consensus with respect to, for example, proper levels of health safety or financial risks to be borne by consumers. This is especially true when policies must be harmonized across jurisdictions such as provinces in Canada or between Canada and the U.S.A. In principle, problems of trade and tradeability could be constrained by regional social differences in assuming and sharing risk between service providers and service consumers.

Regardless of the aforementioned forces toward local monopoly, the introduction of new information technologies in many service sector industries has considerably changed the nature of service provisions. Indeed, the OECDs various studies on the evolution of work and skills in the service sector show that this innovation is the most important force behind the development and use of human resources in this sector. Computerization of activities in both the back and front offices of service providers has changed the mix of industry skills. It has also contributed considerably to the standardization of diagnostic information in the traditional interface between client and service provider (OECD 1986, Mills 1986). This standardization has created an entirely new situation for the international production and trade in services (Dunning 1987). Most of the theories which link locational advantages and technological advances with the changing competitive environment for service industries are eclectic, thus hampering traditional analyses and hypothesis testing. The Economic Council of Canada used in-depth case studies rather than consulting time series of labour market data in its attempt to assess the sources and impact of technological change in the Canadian work environment (ECC 1987).

Summary

Recently, researchers have recognized a multitude of growth determinants in the service economy in addition to the traditional service sector growth explanations of income and price elasticity. The most important among them have been the differential productivity growth between secondary and tertiary sectors, the division of labour and contracting out, the potential for service sector market expansion, trade and social innovation, and the transformation of final service functions. This suggests that the rise of the service economy has been a far more complex phenomenon than it was previously thought to be. One should expect considerable variation of employment growth across different service industries and substantial, ongoing changes in the underlying job and skill structure of the service economy.

NOTES

1. Term used by the French regulation school (see Boyer 1979).

2. Contracting out occurs mainly when other, often smaller, more special-
    ized firms can provide the same service at a lower cost. Cost savings,
    however, do not automatically equate with superior productivity, and
    therefore no definite armour can be provided as to the productivity
    potential of externalization or contracting out.

AN EMPIRICAL ACCOUNT OF
EMPLOYMENT GROWTH IN
CANADIAN SERVICE INDUSTRIES

Chapter 3 brings together empirical evidence on the changing pattern and distribution of employment growth within Canadian service sector industries and contrasts services with the manufacturing sector. Data used is drawn from my own analyses (which use published and unpublished census and labour force survey data) and results reported elsewhere (Picot 1986, ECC 1987). Detailed long-run time series analyses of employment changes are hampered due to the periodic changes in methodology for gathering statistics by federal and provincial agencies with respect to nomenclature, sampling frame, and characteristics composition. For example, employment comparisons between earlier censuses and 1971 or 1981 are rendered extremely difficult, if not entirely meaningless, because of changed industrial and occupational coverage, inclusion and exclusion of specific labour market groups, newly introduced occupational and educational classification systems and the like. Thus, I will concentrate on changes during the past 15 years. Longer term changes can be discerned by comparing 1971 and 1981 census data, since both censuses provide detailed and relatively consistent cross-classified industrial employment data.

Long-Term Evolution and Employment Growth of the Canadian Service Industries

As can be seen from table 1, over the past 35 years the service sector as a whole has steadily increased its share of the labour force from 46 percent in 1951 to 66 percent in 1984. However, these increases have slowed down in relative terms and mask considerable intra-sectoral differences in employment and labour force growth.

Table 1
Experienced Labour Force by Sector, 1951 to 1981

Sector	Experienced Labour Force[1]				Percentage Distribution			
	1951	1961	1971	1981	1951	1961	1971	1981
	(in thousands)							
Agriculture	823.8	637.9	501.0	493.0	15.6	9.9	5.8	4.1
Manufacturing	1,307.1	1,429.9	1,840.0	2,298.0	24.7	22.1	21.3	19.1
Construction	325.4	448.3	580.3	777.3	6.2	6.9	6.7	6.5
Other Goods-Producing	349.8	345.1	355.0	494.7	6.6	5.3	4.1	4.1
Total Goods-Producing	2,806.0	2,861.2	3,276.3	4,063.1	53.1	44.2	38.0	33.8
Distributive Services	1,233.7	1,568.7	2,026.4	2,861.3	23.3	24.2	23.5	23.8
Producer Services	202.8	346.7	621.5	1,134.7	3.8	5.4	7.2	9.5
Consumer Services	387.8	556.8	793.6	1,291.3	7.3	8.6	9.2	10.8
Total Commercial Services	1,824.4	2,472.2	3,441.6	5,287.3	34.5	38.2	39.9	44.0
Non-Commercial Services	656.0	1,138.4	1,909.1	2,654.9	12.4	17.6	22.1	22.1
Total Services	2,480.4	3,610.6	5,350.6	7,942.2	46.0	55.8	62.0	66.2
TOTAL	5,286.4	6,471.8	8,626.9	12,005.3	100.0	100.0	100.0	100.0

Source: G. Picot, 1986, p. 100.

Note: The unclassified industries have been redistributed for all years using the assignment distribution developed for the 1981 Census. All years based on 1970 SIC (Standard Industrial Classification Manual).

By examining secular trends from 1951 to 1981 and using estimates provided by Picot (1986), several changes in percentage shares and rates of growth among the experienced labour force of various service sector aggregates can be identified (see tables 1-3).

Table 2

Changes in Share and Growth Rates of the Experienced Labour Force by Sector

Sector	Changes in Share of Experienced Labour Force			Percentage Change in Experienced Labour Force		
	1951 1961	1961 1971	1971 1981	1951 1961	1961 1971	1971 1981
Agriculture	−5.7	−4.0	−1.7	−22.6	−21.5	−1.6
Manufacturing	−2.6	−0.8	−2.2	9.4	28.7	24.9
Construction	0.8	−0.2	−0.3	37.8	29.4	33.9
Other Goods-Producing	−1.3	−1.2	0.0	−1.3	2.9	39.4
Total Goods-Producing	−8.9	−6.2	−4.1	2.0	14.5	24.0
Distributive Services	0.9	−0.7	0.3	27.2	29.2	41.2
Producer Services	1.6	1.8	2.3	71.0	79.3	82.6
Consumer Services	1.3	0.6	1.6	43.6	42.5	62.7
Total Commercial Services	3.7	1.7	4.1	35.5	39.2	53.6
Non-Commercial Services	5.2	4.5	0.0	73.5	67.7	39.1
Total Services	3.9	6.2	4.1	45.6	48.2	48.4
TOTAL	—	—	—	22.4	33.3	39.2

Source: G. Picot, 1986, p. 101.

Restructuring (as measured by the variance of experienced labour force growth across sectors) was most severe in the 1950s, followed by the 1970s. Labour force growth across all sectors was much more stable during the 1960s.

The distributive services sector (transportation and storage, communication, wholesale and retail trades: SIC 501-548 and 602-699) maintained its share. At the other extreme, producer services (accounting, engineering, legal and management consulting firms, finance, insurance and real estate: SIC 701-737 and 851-869) almost tripled their share from 3.8 percent in

1951 to 9.5 percent in 1981. Social or non-commercial services (education, health and welfare services, religious organizations, public administration: SIC 801-831 and 902-991) saw a rapid increase, doubling their share between 1951 and 1971, but showed no further relative advances in the 1970s. Finally, personal or consumer services (accommodation and food services, amusement and recreational services, and miscellaneous service: SIC 841-849 and 871-899) have experienced the steadiest expansion, with the exception of a stagnant period in the 1960s. Their share has increased in each decade by an average of 1 percent.

Table 3

Percentage of Total Expansion in the Experienced Labour Force Contributed by Each Sector

Sector	1951 1961	1961 1971	1971 1981
Agriculture	−15.7	−6.4	−0.2
Manufacturing	10.4	19.0	13.6
Construction	10.4	6.1	5.8
Other Goods-Producing	−0.4	0.5	4.1
Total Goods-Producing	4.7	19.3	23.3
Distributive Services	28.3	21.2	24.7
Producer Services	12.1	12.8	15.2
Consumer Services	14.3	11.0	14.7
Total Commercial Services	54.6	45.0	54.6
Non-Commercial Services	40.7	35.8	22.1
Total Services	95.3	80.7	76.7
Total Expansion (in thousands)	1,185.4	2,155.1	3,378.4

Source: G. Picot, 1986, p. 102.

Looking at more recent changes between 1981 and 1984 (see tables 4-6), we observe a resumption of above average growth in social or non-commercial services followed by consumer services. The growth in producer services fell, and distributive services decreased. The decline in producer and distributive services was related to the huge downsizing which oc-

Table 4

Industry Changes in Share and Growth Rates in Employment, 1971 to 1984

Industry	Changes in Share of Employment			Percentage Change in Employment		
	Census	L.F. Survey		Census	L.F. Survey	
	1971 1981	1976 1981	1981 1984	1971 1981	1976 1981	1981 1984
Agriculture	−1.8	−0.6	−0.1	−4.6	2.8	−1.9
Forestry	−0.1	0.0	0.0	18.3	11.4	−2.6
Fishing and Trapping	0.0	0.1	0.0	29.2	84.2	−2.9
Mines, Oil, and Gas Wells	0.1	0.4	−0.2	41.1	44.8	−13.3
Food and Beverage	−0.4	−0.2	−0.2	16.0	7.6	−8.6
Tobacco Products	0.0	0.0	−0.1	−9.5	−30.0	−28.6
Rubber and Plastic Products	0.0	0.0	0.1	44.3	19.6	14.9
Leather Industries	−0.1	0.0	0.0	7.2	3.1	−15.2
Textile Industries	−0.2	−0.1	−0.1	10.4	−4.2	−11.8
Knitting Mills	0.0	0.0	−0.1	12.1	0.0	−11.1
Clothing Industries	−0.1	0.0	0.0	19.9	11.7	−4.8
Wood Industries	0.0	0.0	−0.2	38.1	18.8	−15.1
Furniture and Fixture	0.0	0.0	0.0	45.2	13.3	−10.3
Paper and Allied Products	−0.2	−0.2	−0.1	15.0	1.4	−11.7
Printing, Publishing, and Allied	−0.1	0.0	0.1	23.5	17.3	−14.7
Primary Metal	−0.2	0.0	−0.3	14.0	18.0	−19.2
Metal Fabricating (except Machinery and Transportation Equipment)	0.0	0.1	−0.3	33.2	21.1	−22.5
Machinery (except Electrical Machinery)	0.1	0.1	−0.4	48.4	25.0	−37.6
Transportation Equipment	−0.2	−0.2	0.1	22.4	5.9	5.5
Electrical Products	−0.2	−0.1	0.3	12.6	4.6	22.1
Non-Metallic Mineral Products	−0.1	−0.1	−0.1	18.8	−4.6	−14.5
Petroleum, Coal, Chemical and Chemical Products	−0.1	−0.1	0.0	24.7	6.9	−4.8
Miscellaneous Manufacturing Industries	0.0	0.0	0.0	28.5	15.9	0.0
General Contractors	−0.6	−0.6	−0.3	9.9	−7.6	−13.5
Special Trade Contractors	0.4	−0.2	−0.4	50.7	11.0	−11.2

Table 4 —continued

Industry	Changes in Share of Employment			Percentage Change in Employment		
	Census	L.F. Survey		Census	L.F. Survey	
	1971 1981	1976 1981	1981 1984	1971 1981	1976 1981	1981 1984
Transportation and Storage	-0.4	-0.3	-0.5	25.5	9.7	-11.1
Communication	0.1	-0.1	0.1	45.2	10.0	4.5
Electrical Power, Gas and Water Utilities	0.0	0.0	-0.1	41.8	15.3	-3.9
Wholesale Trade	0.5	-0.2	-0.1	50.0	12.2	-1.4
Retail Trade	0.4	-0.1	0.5	40.8	15.5	3.7
Finance Industries	0.5	0.1	0.2	62.5	18.4	6.1
Insurance Carriers	0.0	0.1	0.0	39.0	24.5	1.7
Insurance Agencies and Real Estate	0.4	0.0	0.2	82.2	18.3	9.4
Education and Related	-0.5	-0.5	0.2	27.5	7.4	3.1
Health and Welfare	0.8	0.3	0.8	52.8	21.5	11.2
Religious Organizations	-0.1	0.0	0.2	14.4	18.2	35.4
Amusement and Recreation	0.1	0.2	-0.1	56.4	38.1	-6.7
Services to Business Management	1.5	0.9	0.0	110.7	50.2	1.6
Personal Services	-0.6	0.4	0.2	-3.9	37.1	11.9
Accommodation and Food	1.1	1.1	0.1	71.7	44.5	2.9
Miscellaneous Services	0.6	0.2	0.3	86.0	26.7	14.8
Federal Administration	-0.8	-0.3	0.0	11.3	4.0	-0.4
Provincial Administration	0.2	0.1	0.0	49.7	23.6	2.4
Local Administration and Other Government Offices	0.1	0.0	0.2	46.8	16.6	7.3
TOTAL	—	—	—	36.0	16.1	0.0

Source: G. Picot, 1986, p. 105.

Table 5

Changes in Share and Growth Rates of Employment by Sector, 1971 to 1984

Industry	Changes in Share of Employment			Percentage Change in Employment		
	Census	L.F. Survey		Census	L.F. Survey	
	1971 1981	1976 1981	1981 1984	1971 1981	1976 1981	1981 1984
Agriculture	−1.8	−0.6	−0.1	−4.0	2.8	−1.9
Manufacturing	−2.0	−1.0	−1.4	23.0	10.5	−7.2
Construction	−0.2	−0.8	−0.7	31.0	2.5	−12.1
Other Goods-Producing	0.0	0.5	−0.3	35.5	30.7	−8.0
Total Goods-Producing	−4.1	−1.9	−2.5	21.3	10.0	−7.4
Distributive Services	0.6	−0.7	0.0	39.5	13.1	−0.1
Producer Services	2.4	1.1	0.5	81.4	40.0	4.2
Consumer Services	1.2	1.7	0.7	53.9	38.7	5.9
Total Commercial Services	4.2	2.2	1.1	50.4	22.2	2.3
Non-Commercial Services	−0.1	−0.3	1.4	35.2	14.4	5.8
Total Services	4.1	1.9	2.5	44.9	19.5	3.7
TOTAL	—	—	—	36.0	16.1	−0.1

Source: G. Picot, 1986, p. 108.

curred in the goods-producing sector and which accounted for an employment decline of 7.4 percent.

Before discussing the employment and labour force growth record of the aforementioned service sectors relative to the secular service sector growth models mentioned earlier, we consult employment change data calculated by the Economic Council of Canada in its study on *Innovation and Jobs* (ECC 1987, p. 25). A percentage breakdown of the causes of employment change between 1971 and 1981 for those sectors detailed in the ECC study are listed in table 7.

Baumol's service sector classifications of stagnant personal services, progressive impersonal services and asymptotically stagnant impersonal services (Baumol 1983, 1985) are used to determine the relationship between productivity and employment among various service sector industries (table 7, column 4). As predicted, personal services show only

Table 6

Percentage of Total Expansion in Net Employment Contributed by Each Sector and Changes in Employment

Sector	Percentage of Total Expansion in Net Employment		Change in Employment
	Census 1971–1981	L.F. Survey 1976–1981	L.F. Survey 1981–1984 (in thousands)
Agriculture	−0.8	0.9	−9
Manufacturing	13.5	13.2	−152
Construction	5.5	1.0	−79
Other Goods-Producing	4.0	6.9	−36
Total Goods-Producing	22.3	22.0	−276
Distributive Services	25.7	20.3	−4
Producer Services	16.4	16.1	44
Consumer Services	13.4	22.0	71
Total Commercial Services	55.4	58.4	111
Non-Commercial Services	22.3	19.6	161
Total Services	77.7	78.0	272
TOTAL (in thousands)	2,922	1,529	−6

Source: G. Picot, 1986, p. 109.

small or negative labour productivity trends on account of their resistance to standardization, thereby precluding productivity enhancing changes of employment. Direct contacts between the consumer and those who provide labour inputs have remained important in amusement, recreation, accommodation and food services. Therefore, employment growth derives in large measure from low or negative productivity growth (table 7, column 4). If these services were to become overpriced, they would eventually be substituted by goods (e.g., compact disc for a live performance, ready-to-make gourmet food for restaurant services). This type of service industry also tends to show only low or negative sources of employment growth associated with changes in the pattern of final demand (table 6, column 2).

Table 7

Sources of Employment Change in Industrial Sectors, Canada, 1971–1981

Industry	Share of Employment per Sector	Percent Change in Employment 1971–1981	Level of Final Demand (1)	Pattern of Final Demand (2)	Intermediate Demand (3)	Labour Productivity (4)	Total (1+2+3+4)
Industry Average (all industries)		29.7	131.6	-5.1	7.4	-34.0	100.0
Transportation and Storage	5.5	21.4	182.7	-12.1	6.5	-77.1	100.0
Communications	4.1	37.7	103.7	58.9	72.9	-135.5	100.0
Wholesale Trade	8.0	32.5	120.3	-2.4	-2.7	-15.2	100.0
Retail Trade	25.8	37.6	104.0	-10.5	-7.6	14.1	100.0
Finance, Insurance and Real Estate	13.0	49.1	79.4	14.2	20.2	-13.8	100.0
Education and Health Services	2.5	41.4	94.4	27.8	1.2	-23.4	100.0
Amusement and Recreation Services	2.3	60.9	64.0	43.5	-2.8	-4.7	100.0
Services to Business Management	18.2	74.3	52.6	13.4	66.3	-32.4	100.0
Accommodation and Food Services	12.9	54.0	72.4	2.4	3.0	22.2	100.0
All Other Personal and Miscellaneous Services	7.7	59.4	65.8	-7.0	-3.4	44.6	100.0

Source: *Innovation and Jobs*, p. 25.

Initially, progressively impersonal services experience accelerated productivity growth. As the initial sources of productivity growth become invalid, however, secular stagnation results. Baumol cites the example of the computation and information processing industry where tremendous productivity gains have been made in hardware development. The development and installation of more labour intensive software is now becoming dominant. Sectors which appear to fit this description most closely are business services, education, health services, and financial services.[1] As can be seen from table 7, these service sectors are characterized by large productivity-related declines in employment which were, however, balanced by relatively large employment increases due to changes in the pattern of final and intermediate demand. Finally, transportation, storage, and communications typically represent progressive impersonal services with high productivity growth. In this group, negative employment effects from productivity are more than offset by changes in final demand and intermediate demand growth.

Before fitting these observations into the service sector growth debate, it may also be useful to consider the relative share that each of the service sectors occupied in the total expansion of employment between the two censuses. Of the service sector in total, which in itself accounted for over 80 percent of all employment expansion between 1971 and 1981, the percentage split among the three commercial service sectors was as follows:

DISTRIBUTIVE SERVICES		
transportation and storage	5.5	
communication	4.1	
wholesale and retail trade	33.8	43.4
CONSUMER SERVICES		
accommodation and food	12.9	
amusement and recreation	2.3	
all others	7.7	22.9
PRODUCER SERVICES		
services to business management	18.2	
finance, insurance, and real estate	13.0	31.2
EDUCATION, HEALTH AND WELFARE		.5
TOTAL		100.0

Source: Calculated from tables 4 and 6.

Although producer and distributive services account for the lion's share in this intercensal comparison (over 74 percent of the total employment expansion), they also appear to be more directly connected to the manufacturing sector than the other services are. Two observations support this claim: the slowdown in the expansion of producer and distributive services employment during the downsizing of the manufacturing sector between 1981 and 1984 (see table 5) and the relatively higher correlations with employment growth in manufacturing in comparison to other services such as personal and social services (see table 8). Given the stronger interplay of economic forces between services and goods producing industries, there are *a priori* reasons for establishing correlations between manufacturing and the service sectors. Nevertheless, it should be pointed out that correlations cannot prove causality. Far more complex modelling is necessary to establish the exact nature of relationships between manufacturing and service sector output and employment growth.

Table 8

Correlation Coefficients for Annual Employment Growth in Various Service Sectors and Annual Employment Growth in Manufacturing 1970–1982

Manufacturing and Total Service Sector	.75
Manufacturing and Distributive Services	.84
Manufacturing and Producer Services	.72
Manufacturing and Personal Services	.60
Manufacturing and Non-Commercial Services	.62

Source: Own calculations from unpublished industry employment statistics provided by Statistics Canada.

In light of the discussion in chapter 2 and our limited empirical evidence on the determination of secular changes in services employment, the following tentative conclusions are reached: the initial phase of massive and rapid service sector expansion is slowing down; and future growth will be much more limited to the growth of stagnant personal and progressively impersonal services. These, in turn, will create jobs because of lagging productivity growth and the lack of goods substitution.

To the extent that Canadian service industries become internationally competitive and trade barriers for services decrease, there is a further possibility for the expansion of service sector employment. Nevertheless, the scanty empirical evidence that we have points to much slower overall future growth and, as such, confirms the more pessimistic outlook of Petit (1986) and others (e.g., Magun 1982). It also compares favourably with the results from a recent Statistics Canada study which concluded "that the overall change in employment between 1981 and 1984 was mainly due to the decline in the goods producing sector rather than a rapidly growing service sector" (Picot 1986, p. 25).

The Secular Trend Towards Part-Time and Contractual Work in the Service Sector

Tables 9 and 10 show the changing composition of full- and part-time employment and the growth in both employment categories for major service sectors and the manufacturing sector over the past ten years.

Table 9

The Share of Part-Time Workers in Major Service Sectors and in the Manufacturing Sector, 1976–1986

Sectors	1976	1978	1980	1982	1984	1986
Transportation, Communication and Other Utilities	4.5	4.6	5.5	5.2	5.6	6.3
Trade (Wholesale and Retail)	20.9	21.4	22.7	23.4	23.9	23.4
Finance, Insurance and Real Estate	6.7	8.2	8.8	9.5	11.1	12.0
Community, Business and Personal Service Industries	18.1	20.0	21.7	22.7	24.4	24.9
Public Administration and Defence	4.5	5.2	5.2	4.9	5.9	7.7
Manufacturing Industries	2.6	2.8	2.9	3.4	3.5	3.8

Source: Statistics Canada, catalogue 71-001, various years.

Table 10

Percentage Rate of Employment Growth Among Full-Time and Part-Time Workers in the Service Sector, 1976–1985

	1976–1981		1981–1985	
	Full-Time	Part-Time	Full-Time	Part-Time
Transportation, Communication and Other Utilities	7.1	23.7	0.9	23.4
Trade (Wholesale and Retail)	9.2	23.4	12.3	14.5
Finance, Insurance and Real Estate	15.0	69.7	7.9	39.3
Community, Business and Personal Services	20.5	60.8	11.7	25.4
Public Administration	7.5	21.9	2.6	59.0
Manufacturing Industries	9.7	5.7	-6.8	-5.0

Source: Statistics Canada, catalogue 71-001, various years.

In comparison with manufacturing, part-time employment grew much faster in the financial industries, personal and business services and, a more distant third, public administration. This is illustrated in the tables by the changing share of full- and part-time employment and the varying rates of employment growth for part- and full-time employment in the service sector. Female employment growth accounts for most of the secular expansion of part-time employment in the service sector, as can be seen from the varying share of male and female full- and part-time employment in 1975 and 1983. Female employment growth has been much stronger in part-time than in full-time jobs. This has led to a larger part-time employment share of female workers in most service sector industries in 1983 than in 1975. A similar phenomenon could be observed in the manufacturing sector. An interesting exception has been the financial services sector, which experienced a more rapid growth of full-time female jobs, thus transferring previous part-time work into full-time work.

The secular rise of part-time work and the larger share of women than men in part-time employment growth has been a pervasive phenomenon in many sectors of the economy. It can also be found in many other industrialized countries (Weiermair 1987). Given its prominence in the Canadian economy, it has been the subject of national inquiries and special studies (Reid 1983, Reid and Swartz 1982, Labour Canada 1983). The substitution of part-time for full-time labour in employment is a fairly complex phenomenon resulting from both fundamental change on the supply side— the secular rise of labour force participation rates of married females and youths attending school; the changing opportunity costs of work and leisure; the income effects in labour supply decisions; and changing worker preferences regarding working time and working time flexibility (Weiermair 1987, p. 8)—and from greater fluctuations in sales and production, and higher productivity and lower labour costs of part-time workers on the demand side (Labour Canada 1983). Since these changes have been dealt with in detail elsewhere, only those aspects which relate to differences between the service sector and other sectors of the Canadian economy will be discussed here.

As will be shown subsequently, the service sector employs a disproportionate share of female and young workers in relation to the other sectors of the economy. Students and females, particularly married female workers, are known to have a much higher probability of being in the part-time as opposed to the full-time labour force (Labour Canada 1983, pp. 46-54). The high incidence of part-time employment in service industries can therefore be identified as being related to the employment problems of student and female, mainly married female, labour.

Citing varying demographics begs the question as to their prevalence in the service sector. Three arguments, one supply side and two demand side can be advanced. On the supply side, it can be argued that the increased flexibility of working time and increased availability of part-time work have stimulated labour force participation rates and hours of work offered by students and married females. It should be pointed out however, that spouses and family members' inter-dependencies and simultaneity in decision making concerning market and non-market activities (work, schooling and leisure) so far have prevented rigourous modelling of labour supply functions (Kosters 1966, Knieser 1976).

On the demand side, one of the most frequently cited reasons for the heavier use of part-time labour in the service sector is the variability of product demand due to extended business hours and seasonal peaks in most retail and service businesses. The second, almost as frequently cited reason for employers' preferences for part-time workers, stems from observations of higher productivity and lower wages among part-time workers (see for example, Labour 1983, p. 119 ff.). Finally, use of part-time workers in the service sector may be greatly facilitated by the low rates of union penetration in this sector. Canadian unions have traditionally been concerned with and have objected to the employment of part-time and contractual labour (ILO 1973, Labour Canada 1983).

Evidence with respect to the strength of the aforementioned determinants is rather sketchy and circumstantial. As to the relationship of part-time to full-time pay, studies undertaken by a variety of government agencies suggest ratios of 0.67 to 0.98, depending on the specific service industry in question and inclusion of fringe benefits (Statistics Canada 1972, 1973; Labour Canada 1983, p. 164), thus attesting to the lower cost of part-time labour relative to full-time labour.

Table 11

Average Hourly Earnings in Paid Worker Jobs

(in dollars)

	Total Full-Time and Part-Time	Both Sexes		Men		Women	
		Full-Time	Part-Time	Full-Time	Part-Time	Full-Time	Part-Time
Total	8.52	8.64	6.84	9.39	7.24	7.27	6.66
Full Year	8.98	9.08	7.26	9.83	8.05	7.66	6.95
Part Year	7.29	7.41	6.25	8.10	6.31	6.31	6.22
Union	9.59	9.60	9.41	10.07	10.47	8.56	8.93
Non-Union	7.87	8.03	6.19	8.91	6.41	6.61	6.09

Source: Statistics Canada, Survey of 1981 Work History, (unpublished).

Similarly (as can be seen from table 11), a positive correlation exists between pay (both full-time and part-time) and the level of unionization. The latter suggests that earnings in the service sector industries should be lower because of both the larger share of part-time, particularly female part-time workers, and the known lower levels of unionization in this sector.

The importance of extended business hours and, more generally, the greater variability in output and sales and associated part-time employment can probably best be gauged by international comparisons (see table 12) which show a much greater share of part-time labour in service sectors in Canada and the U.S.A. than in Europe where business hours appear to be more regulated.

Table 12

Percentage Distribution of Part-Time Workers by Economic Activity

(Both Sexes)

Major Industry Division

Country	Year	Primary	Manufacturing	Construction	Trade Finance Services	Other	All
Australia	(1980)	6.8	7.2	4.7	78.5	2.8	100
Canada	(1981)	6.3	4.8	2.6	86.2	0.1	100
Denmark	(1981)	5.2	8.9	1.8	83.9	0.2	100
France	(1981)	14.4	8.4	3.6	72.3	1.3	100
Germany	(1981)	9.2	18.0	2.8	69.5	0.5	100
Italy	(1981)	25.8	16.9	4.0	53.1	0.2	100
Japan	(1980)	23.0	21.2	6.5	48.8	0.5	100
Norway	(1978)	8.9	13.2	2.1	72.2	0.6	100
U.K.	(1981)	2.5	13.0	1.4	82.3	0.8	100
U.S.A.	(1981)	n.a.	5.6	1.7	92.7	—	100

Source: OECD, 1983, p. 50.

Finally, the supply-side variables may not be as strong as initially assumed. Evidence from the survey of 1981 work history carried out by Statistics Canada indicates that over 32 percent of male part-time employees and over 25 percent of female part-time employees wanted to work additional hours in 1981 (Labour Canada 1983, p. 69). Similarly, the share of involuntary part-time employment has been steadily rising since 1976 (Dumas 1986).

Given the much greater prevalence of part-time work in the service sector, shorter term contractual relations, expressed in terms of job tenure,

Table 13

Job Tenure by Industry, 1975 and 1983

Industry	1–3 Months 1975	1983	4–6 Months 1975	1983	7–12 Months 1975	1983	1–5 Years 1975	1983	6–10 Years 1975	1983	11–20 Years 1975	1983	Over 20 Years 1975	1983
Manufacturing	7.9	7.5	5.7	5.0	8.3	5.3	29.7	28.5	16.6	20.6	15.7	20.6	16.1	12.5
Transportation, Communication and Utilities	7.4	5.3	4.6	3.7	7.4	4.5	27.7	26.9	16.4	22.0	16.7	22.1	19.8	15.5
Trade	10.9	9.6	8.4	7.2	11.5	8.8	34.5	37.9	14.2	17.2	11.5	13.0	9.0	6.3
Finance, Insurance and Real Estate	7.9	5.4	6.9	4.7	11.6	7.8	37.1	38.4	15.8	21.9	11.6	14.8	9.1	7.0
Services	11.9	10.9	8.3	7.2	10.6	8.7	34.3	34.6	17.1	17.4	10.9	16.0	6.9	5.2
Public Administration	8.8	7.7	5.4	4.3	7.7	4.6	29.3	27.4	17.7	22.8	17.0	22.3	14.1	10.9

Source: Statistics Canada, catalogue 71-001, various years.

should be expected. Table 13 shows the distribution of job tenure for manufacturing and various service sectors for the years 1975 and 1983. Two observations emerge. First, job tenure is indeed shorter in the service sectors as compared to manufacturing. For example in 1975, only 22 percent of the work-force in manufacturing had job tenure of one year or less, while 31 percent in trade and services fell in this minimal tenure category. Similarly, over 16 percent of the work-force in manufacturing had job tenure of 20 years or more compared to 7 and 9 percent in services and trade.

Although the service sector still shows a larger proportion of its work-force with shorter job tenure in 1983, these differences narrowed between 1975 and 1983. A general interpretation of the job tenure data suggests that while the service sector displays on average a relatively shorter term job structure compared to the manufacturing sector, this relationship has not changed much over time. If anything, differences have become smaller, implying that service sector industries have followed and responded to common labour supply trends.

According to the 1981 Statistics Canada Work History Survey on multiple job holdings, the majority of persons who held two jobs had at least one position in a service industry (73.7 percent) but only 36.8 percent had both jobs in services. One-third of all multiple job holders worked in community and related services (health and welfare and education) followed by the wholesale and retail industry which accounted for 29.1 percent of all multiple job holdings (Duchesne 1985, p. 15 ff). Thus, the service sector generated multiple job holders and provided additional jobs to a far greater extent than any other sector.

The Age and Sex Distribution of Employment

A detailed breakdown of longer term employment changes by age and sex in various service sector industries can be gained from 1971 and 1981 census figures. Tables 14 and 15 show the percentage growth of employment for both males and females for the age categories 15-19, 20-24, 25-44, and 45 and over, for 21 service industry groups and for the total manufacturing sector covering the period 1971 to 1981.

Although there is considerable variation in age related employment growth across different service industries, the service sector as a whole and most of its subsectors show a growth pattern which is substantially different from the manufacturing sector.

Considering the combined male and female employment growth (table 14), the most striking difference is the big increase in teenage employment in such sectors as trade and community, business and personal service, and of those over 45 years of age in the financial, business, and community and

Table 14

Growth Rates of Employment, by Age, by Service Sector Industry, 1971–1981

Industry	15–19	20–24	25–44	45 +
Manufacturing Industries	26.2	42.3	40.4	17
Transport, Communications and Other Utilities	51.15	49.88	58.37	19.18
Transportation	32.68	58.83	46.59	11.6
Storage	53.21	84.92	48.56	4.45
Communications	2.36	37.55	84.19	34.15
Electric Power, Gas and Water Utilities	34.23	40.74	66.05	36.83
Trade	74.77	80.37	67.2	19.8
Wholesale Trade	81.5	81.69	74.78	27.66
Retail Trade	73.69	79.84	63.65	16.85
Finance, Insurance and Real Estate	37.47	50.88	112.9	41.54
Finance Industries	34.77	48.34	116.25	34.58
Insurance Carriers	10.8	32.02	75.18	24.54
Insurance Agencies and Real Estate Industry	90.23	87.95	134.41	54.2
Community, Business and Personal Service Industries	92.42	41.23	92.97	30.3
Education and Related Services	4.91	–41.9	61.78	35.31
Health and Welfare Services	18.85	24.52	113.59	36.79
Religious Organizations	25	49.4	35.08	4.99
Amusement and Recreation Services	100.54	96.53	116.2	6.7
Services to Business Management	133.12	131.2	163.43	70.42
Personal Services	–13.66	11.69	28.35	–25.3
Accommodation and Food Services	194.92	181.19	89.41	22.86
Miscellaneous Services	147.8	138.12	138.38	56.51
Public Administration and Defence	20.98	19.42	63.61	16.39
Federal Administration	–2.56	6.74	36.93	2.29
Provincial Administration	5.46	19.66	113.63	28.41
Local Administration	112.03	52.79	76.44	31.34
Other Government Offices	–27.27	–32.14	–24.12	–23.03

Source: Census Canada, 1971 and 1981.

Table 15

Employment Growth in Service Sector Industries by Age and Sex, 1971–1981

Growth Rates for Employed Labour Force

Industry	15–19		20–24		25–44		45 +	
	Male	Female	Male	Female	Male	Female	Male	Female
Manufacturing Industries	30.6	18.1	39.3	49.7	30.5	76.1	11.2	40.1
Transport, Communications and Other Utilities	36.59	25.87	42.86	65.53	42.2	151.2	13	66.3
Transportation	39.39	104.39	45.57	119.13	32.3	188.3	6.7	87.5
Storage	64.2	21.43	78.15	112.63	38.1	130.5	–0.3	46
Communications	24.74	–8.54	37.9	37.24	66	122.7	24.9	54.5
Electric Power, Gas and Water Utilities	27.88	49.39	32.33	64.45	54.7	164.2	3,434	64.8
Trade	58.51	98.45	55.57	4,126.68	48.2	106.8	7.5	38.6
Wholesale Trade	84.83	74.96	72.65	102.8	59.6	135.14	18.9	63.8
Retail Trade	53.71	101.36	47.99	134.46	41.2	99.8	0.9	34.7
Finance, Insurance and Real Estate	55.6	34.02	3.24	70.21	58.6	177.7	183.4	85.5
Finance Industries	26.74	36.09	–10.67	71.01	51.2	175.2	–2.8	94.2
Insurance Carriers	21.51	–3.37	–12.71	50.19	26.2	155.2	11.9	48
Insurance Agencies and Real Estate Industry	108.66	82.63	71.34	96.3	94	201.6	36.6	93.7

Table 15—Continued

Industry	15–19		20–24		25–44		45 +	
	Male	Female	Male	Female	Male	Female	Male	Female
Community, Business and Personal Service Industries	121.65	77.33	48.67	37.8	66.1	116	24.5	35
Education and Related Services	14.14	0.34	-41.16	-42.2	36.1	86.9	41.5	30.4
Health and Welfare Services	58.75	10.04	32.7	22.9	76.7	126.4	15.6	46.1
Religious Organizations	26.17	23.74	55.44	44.2	19.6	62.1	-3.8	14.6
Amusement and Recreation Services	72.13	141.9	57.66	185.4	93.4	160.3	-11.7	49.9
Services to Business Management	131.65	134.05	100.82	162.4	129.7	237.3	57.6	102.6
Personal Services	-1.34	-416.04	-4.71	16.6	-2.6	48	-32.6	-21.4
Accommodations and Food Services	210.83	184.77	143.52	209.1	64.6	110.1	16.9	27.2
Miscellaneous Services	122.86	195.87	118.96	167.1	100.6	212.5	0.59	98.4
Public Administration and Defence	5.4	45.18	-8.83	71.6	34	171.6	8.5	41.7
Federal Administration	-12.5	18.81	-16.31	57.6	9.9	136.7	-5.5	23.8
Provincial Administration	-9.98	16.87	-20.78	61.9	73.8	207.7	16.3	60.7
Local Administration	78	167.82	80.83	146.1	53.1	226.9	25.4	67.7
Other Government Offices	-25	-28.57	-28.57	-34.3	-60.5	24.7	-47.8	48.7

Source: Census Canada, 1971 and 1981.

personal services sectors. In many cases, the growth in teenage and older worker employment has been double, triple, and even quadruple that of the manufacturing sector as a whole.

Particularly noteworthy in absorbing teenagers—the largest growing labour force segment of the seventies—were wholesale trade, retail trade, insurance and real estate agencies, business services, accommodation and food services, miscellaneous services, and local government. Relative to the 26.2 percent employment growth of the manufacturing sector, these services increased their employment by 81.5, 73.7, 90.2, 100.6, 133.1, 194.9, 147.8 and 112 percent, respectively. As distinct from other age categories of employment growth and with the exception of retail trade and local government employment, employment growth in these categories has also been evenly distributed between the sexes.

With respect to employment of persons aged 25-44 and those 45 years and older, differences between manufacturing and the service sector have been less striking. In both cases, female employment outgrew male employment on average by two to one. Adult female employment has shown particularly high growth rates both in absolute terms and in relation to male employment growth in such service industries as transportation, communication and utilities, and the financial, insurance and real estate sectors as well as public administration. Overall, the service sector as a whole (versus the goods-producing sector) appears to have absorbed a larger number of adult females (25 and above) which, due to secularly rising female labour force participation rates, represented the second fastest growing labour force segment in the seventies.

Although the business services sector averaged higher employment growth potential for women, it showed gains for all sex and age categories, demonstrating the tremendous expansion of these industries.

With the exception of education and related services, which (in all age categories) showed an intercensal lowering of the female employment share relative to males, all the other 20 service sectors experienced an increase in the share of female employment for all age categories. The latter portrays the secular feminization of the service sector.

Although less detailed employment data are available for the eighties, the trends which were set in motion in the seventies have hardly changed.

Self-Employment and Business Formation in the Service Sector

Two previous Statistics Canada surveys (catalogue 18-501 and 71-582) and unpublished statistical material on job creation in Canada from the Department of Regional Economic Expansion form the basis of the following analysis.

Table 16
Employment by Class of Worker, Industry, and Percentage of Self-Employed Workers
Annual Averages, Canada, 1984

	Total of Workers (in thousands)	Self-Employed Workers Relative to Total Employment (percentage)	Own Account Self-Employed	Employers
All Industries	1,480	13.50	56.1	43.9
Agriculture	266	55.80	76.1	23.9
Other Primary	38	13.00	57.3	42.7
Manufacturing	74	3.70	24.9	75.1
Construction	166	29.00	47	53
Transportation, Communications and Utilities	68	7.90	63.8	36.2
Trade	327	17.00	45.3	54.7
Finance, Insurance and Real Estate	49	7.70	43.2	56.8
Community, Business and Personal Services	492	14.10	60.5	39.5

Source: Statistics Canada, catalogue 71-582, p. 15.

According to a Statistics Canada survey in 1984, over half a million people were self-employed. The distribution of self-employed across sectors, their percentage share in relation to total employment in the respective sectors, and the partition between own account workers and employers among the self-employed are shown in table 16.

In absolute terms, the service sector employs 63.2 percent of all self-employed workers which is in line with this sector's share of total employment. Self-employment, however, is considerably higher in relative terms in such sectors as agriculture and construction. Only manufacturing shows a substantially lower share of self-employed workers relative to the service sector. In the personal, business and community services, and transportation, communication and utility sectors, own account workers constitute the majority among the self-employed. The distribution between employees and own account workers is more even in the remaining service sectors— trade, finance, and real estate and insurance.

Turning to business formation, enterprise turnover and job creation in the service sector, the following pertinent observations based on tables 17 and 18 can be made. In light of the negative employment growth of manufacturing and construction between 1976 and 1984, the net employment change, amounting to over half a million jobs, was accounted for by the employment growth of the service sector. As can be seen from table 19, there is a clear bimodal distribution of employment change with the very large (500+) and the very small (0-19) enterprises accounting for all the job

Table 17

Net Change in Employment by Industry, 1976 to 1984

Components of Change Expressed as a Percentage of 1976 Base Employment

Industry	Net Change	Birth	Death	Expansion	Contraction
Agriculture	22.1	35.4	24.6	23.6	12.3
Forestry	6.9	43.0	37.5	18.1	16.7
Fishing	19.8	40.1	22.7	22.7	20.3
Mines	18.3	47.4	31.7	18.7	16.1
Manufacturing	−3.3	27.3	32.2	14.6	12.9
Construction	−14.6	31.4	39.4	13.4	20.1
Transport	16.2	37.6	26.9	21.9	16.4
Trade	7.4	38.1	35.4	16.0	11.3
Finance	13.7	42.7	35.5	21.1	14.6
Services	26.7	40.4	25.3	20.9	9.3
TOTAL	8.0	35.2	31.8	17.3	12.7

Source: Department of Regional Industrial Expansion, Statistical Analysis, *A Study of Job Creation in Canada, 1976–1984*, p. 17.

Table 18

Percentage Distribution of Net Employment Change in Service Industries, 1976 to 1984, by Enterprise Size within Industry

Industry	Enterprise Employment Size Group							Number of Employees
	0–19	20–49	50–99	100–199	200–499	500 +	Total	
Agriculture	98.5	4.1	0.0	-6.2	-3.5	7.1	100.0	10,039
Forestry	112.8	-40.5	-15.9	-63.5	11.3	95.8	100.0	1,895
Fishing	196.0	-19.2	-6.6	13.3	-39.5	-44.0	100.0	772
Mines	40.0	5.0	3.8	2.3	3.4	45.6	100.0	19,821
Manufacturing	-126.1	-12.3	33.6	83.0	108.5	13.3	100.0	-52,979
Construction	-20.1	32.9	29.3	31.9	15.6	10.4	100.0	-64,288
Transport	38.1	0.8	-2.6	-8.2	-0.9	72.9	100.0	56,536
Trade	102.8	-2.3	-14.7	-20.2	-9.0	43.4	100.0	90,141
Finance	58.6	16.2	5.4	-3.6	-5.1	28.6	100.0	42,348
Services	41.5	12.2	7.1	4.4	1.3	33.4	100.0	325,692
TOTAL	87.3	7.2	-5.9	-17.6	-17.1	46.2	100.0	429,977

Source: Department of Regional Industrial Expansion, Statistical Analysis, *A Study of Job Creation in Canada 1976–1984*, p. 14.

Table 19

Percentage Distribution of Net Employment Change in Service Industries, 1976 to 1984, by Enterprise Size within Sector

Sector	Enterprise Employment Size Group						Total	Number of Employees
	0–19	20–49	50–99	100–199	200–499	500+		
Education	15.1	3.4	-0.6	6.9	17.8	57.4	100.0	28,060
Museums	73.6	4.2	-2.3	22.5	-3.4	5.5	100.0	1,224
Health	14.3	5.5	4.2	4.7	6.7	64.7	100.0	55,531
Social	36.2	26.5	11.5	8.9	5.3	11.7	100.0	8,854
Religion	224.9	62.9	52.7	-140.1	-161.6	61.2	100.0	237
Amusement/Recreation	67.8	15.3	10.0	4.7	-2.4	4.6	100.0	16,107
Business	34.7	11.0	4.5	8.1	2.5	39.2	100.0	29,727
Professional Services	48.4	9.6	4.9	3.5	4.0	29.6	100.0	62,378
Personal Services	1,307.4	-208.3	-377.7	-336.4	-617.4	332.2	100.0	242
Accommodation	42.9	23.7	17.3	5.1	-3.8	14.9	100.0	88,061
Miscellaneous Services	73.9	3.2	-1.0	0.3	-7.0	30.6	100.0	35,271
TOTAL	41.5	12.2	7.1	4.4	1.3	33.4	100.0	692

Source: Department of Regional Industrial Expansion, Statistical Analysis, *A Study of Job Creation in Canada*, p. 22.

Table 20

Employment Changes by Firm Size in the Major Groups of Community Services and Business and Personal Services, 1978 to 1982

Industry	Employment				
	1978	1982	Net Change 1978–82	Rate of Change %	% Share in Job Creation
Education and Related	624,996	689,526	64,530	10.3	31.0
Health and Welfare	591,128	729,688	138,560	23.4	66.6
Religious Organizations	32,472	37,312	4,840	14.9	2.3
Community Services	1,248,596	1,456,526	207,930	16.6	100.0
Amusement and Recreation	81,998	93,748	11,750	14.3	5.6
Services to Business Management	354,546	434,154	79,608	22.5	38.0
Personal Services	75,292	88,261	12,969	17.2	6.2
Accommodation and Food	516,572	576,212	59,641	11.5	28.5
Miscellaneous Services	170,742	216,380	45,639	26.7	21.8
Business and Personal Services	1,199,150	1,408,757	209,607	17.5	100.0

Industry	Rates of Change (%) by Firm Size					
	Less than 5	5 to Less than 20	20 to Less than 50	50 to Less than 100	100 to Less than 500	500 or More
Education and Related	293.4	118.3	4.9	2.4	16.8	4.9
Health and Welfare	81.2	37.2	25.8	25.4	18.7	16.6
Religious Organizations	15.3	14.9	7.1	10.5	X	X
Community Services	78.0	48.5	25.3	18.3	17.7	9.6
Amusement and Recreation	39.1	7.0	1.0	10.9	26.6	0.3
Services to Business Management	78.7	19.7	14.1	14.2	14.3	7.7
Personal Services	44.7	3.0	−2.5	2.2	18.7	7.8
Accommodation and Food	67.5	9.7	3.5	7.6	6.8	4.7
Miscellaneous Services	63.1	27.0	14.7	8.9	60.9	5.3
Business and Personal Services	64.6	13.5	6.5	9.5	18.5	5.7

Source: Department of Regional Economic Expansion, Statistical and Data Base Services (1985), An Analysis of Job Creation based on the T4 Employment Estimates Data Base 1978–82.

Note: "X" indicates data not available due to confidentiality.

creation. This also suggests some interesting hypotheses about competitive advantages and survival chances of service sector businesses, which will be explored later.

Looking at the variation among types of employment changes in terms of contraction, death, expansion and birth of enterprises (table 17), there are few statistically significant differences between broad sectors. The only emerging observation seems to be a slightly stronger expansion and weaker contraction pattern in the service sector pointing to the greater relative cyclical stability of this sector. In terms of specific service sector industries, we may want to analyse the community, personal and business services sector for which more dissegregated data were available (see tables 19 and 20).

Using a different time frame, for example 1978 to 1982, and looking at firm turnover as opposed to general employment turnover (table 21), the following observations can be made. Business services displayed the highest rate of corporate turnover, typical of dynamic industries. Community services, which includes a fair number of public institutions, on the other hand, displayed a much greater stability of jobs and firms, thus yielding much lower firm turnover rates. And, generally speaking, manufacturing industries show less firm turnover in comparison to service sector industries which may, to a large measure, result from the very different size distribution of firms in those two sectors.

Another interesting phenomenon worth reporting in the context of a discussion on corporate turnover and job creation is the differential cyclical behaviour of independent and dependent work. According to results from the survey on self-employment in Canada, the number of self-employed workers grew by 6.2 percent while the number of paid workers fell by 4.7 percent over the period from December 1980 to December 1982 which marked Canada's sharpest and longest post-war recession (Statistics Canada 1985, p. 20). During the recession, most of this increase was the result of growth among employers. Later, during the first phase of business expansion, paid worker employment grew by 5.9 percent in comparison to 9.5 percent for self-employed workers. However, at this time, the dominant engine of employment growth was the category of own account workers (Statistics Canada 1985, pp. 20 and 21).

Table 22 shows employment changes classified by sex, age, and industry during the 1981 recession and the subsequent upswing from 1982 to 1984 for the 16 largest groups of self-employed workers. As expected, the largest numerical increase occurred in the category of self-employed service sector adult workers with women registering a higher percentage increase than men. Female entrepreneurs appeared to be particularly prevalent in such sectors as accommodation and food, household and personal services (a phenomenon which is further explained by changing participation rates of

Table 21
Components of Change in the Number of Firms by Industry, 1978 to 1982

Industry	Number of Firms					
	Births	Deaths	Continuous	Birth Rate	Death Rate	Turnover Rate
Primary	34,145	–16,754	30,175	72.8	–35.7	108.5
Mining	1,947	–983	2,325	58.9	–29.7	88.6
Manufacturing	14,651	–10,794	29,526	36.3	–26.8	63.1
Construction	31,437	–31,753	48,256	39.3	–39.7	79.0
Transportation	12,615	–9,308	16,691	48.5	–35.8	84.3
Wholesale Trade	15,553	–11,407	28,795	38.7	–28.4	67.1
Retail Trade	52,252	–39,586	72,613	46.6	–35.3	81.9
Finance	16,489	–12,526	27,196	41.5	–31.5	73.0
Community Services	17,131	–8,181	40,367	35.3	–16.9	52.1
Business Services	106,669	–61,115	87,243	76.1	–43.6	119.7
TOTAL	327,167	–211,583	384,846	54.9	–35.5	90.3

Source: Department of Regional Economic Expansion, Statistical Analysis Policy, 1986, Firm Adjustment and Employment Turnover 1978–82, table 6.

Table 22

Change in the Number of Self-Employed Workers by Age, Sex, and Industry, December 1980 to December 1982 and December 1982 to December 1984

(in thousands)

	December 1980	December 1982	December 1984	Change December 1980/ December 1982	Change December 1982/ December 1984
Males 25 years and over, Services	196	231	251	36	20
Males 25 years and over, Agriculture	228	205	215	-23	10
Males 25 years and over, Trade and Commerce	197	197	210	—	13
Females 25 years and over, Services	138	159	193	20	35
Males 25 years and over, Construction	135	153	153	18	—
Females 25 years and over, Trade and Commerce	72	71	93	-13	21
Females 15–24 years, Services	59	65	72	7	6
Males 25 years and over, Transportation and Transport	58	54	54	-43	—
Males 25 years and over, Manufacturing and Industries	58	59	64	1	5
Males 25 years and over, Finance, Insurance and Real Estate	32	33	37	1	4
Males 25 years and over, Other Primary Industries	24	33	31	9	-23
Females 25 years and over, Agriculture	21	30	35	9	5
Males 15–24 years, Trade and Commerce	18	23	29	5	5
Males 15–24 years, Services	13	17	17	5	-13
Males 15–24 years, Agriculture	10	10	13	—	3
Others	56	55	64	-23	9
TOTAL	1,316	1,397	1,530	81	132

Source: Statistics Canada, 1985, Self-Employment in Canada, catalogue 71-582, table 5, p. 22.

married females), sex-related comparative advantages, or previous labour force experience, lower earnings and profit expectations among women, and low entry barriers for many service sector businesses (Belcourt and Weiermair 1987).

Similarly, it is worthwhile to point out the increased self-employment among youth (15-24) in the trade and services sector during the recession (table 22). Thus, economic downturns appear to cause a shift from laid-off paid workers to self-employment in a reallocation process which mainly involves females and service sector industries. The latter is in line with earlier observations of the feminization of service sector industries and the greater cyclical stability of service sector employment. It is also in line with research reporting increases in business formation during recessions.

Summary

The empirical evidence of changes in employment in the service sector over the past 15 years supports the opinion that growth in this sector has been due to a variety of factors and not merely a result of price and income elasticities. The significant variances in growth rates across the different classifications of service sector industries are due to various elements in the changing demand for and nature of service sector jobs.

From various analyses of the available data, the period of rapid expansion of the service sector may be coming to an end. Assuming trends continue, future growth rates will be much lower and will be limited, in Baumol's terminology, to stagnant personal services and progressively impersonal services. Elements of the changing nature of service sector employment for which there is strong empirical evidence include the rise of part-time work, especially among women and youth, and the large increase in self-employment. Indeed, in the recent past, entrepreneurship has come to be considered a purely service sector phenomenon. Finally, the secular rise of part-time work in service sector industries, the relatively shorter job duration in this sector, the greater incidence of multiple job holdings involving service industries, and its greater proportion of youth employment indicate high levels of labour market flexibility in service sector industries. In turn this suggests a relative ease in the short-run adjustment and allocation of labour in this sector.

NOTE

1. There are of course considerable behavioural variations within these given service sectors.

Chapter 4

ON THE CHANGING NATURE OF
JOBS IN THE SERVICE SECTOR

Over the past 20 years large segments of the service sector in most industrialized countries have experienced technological change, notably in the form of new information technologies. This has resulted in altered forms of work organization and created new skills, occupations, and careers. Because of the massive industrial restructuring in the tertiary sector, a considerable amount of research has recently been directed toward the study of technological change and human resource development in the service sector. Notably the OECD, through its Centre for Educational Research and Innovation, has carried out or commissioned case studies on the impact of recent computerization on work organization, skills, and personnel training in service sector industries in the U.S.A., Japan, West Germany, France, and Sweden (OECD/CERI 1987).

While there are no comparably comprehensive studies for Canada, some of the evidence can be pieced together from a recent study of innovation and changes in jobs across all Canadian industries (ECC 1987), from provincial studies and task forces on employment and new technologies (Ontario Task Force on Employment and New Technology 1985, and Ontario Study of the Service Sector 1986) specific studies on the introduction of microcomputers (Menzies 1981 and Labour Canada 1982), and various published and unpublished case studies and consultants' reports on technological change. In addition, comparisons between the 1971 and 1981 censuses showing changes in the distribution of educational attainment and occupational characteristics of employment in the service sector should further help in gathering empirical evidence, albeit circumstantial, on the changing nature of service sector jobs.

Changing Production Functions in the Service Economy

Major changes which service sector industries had to face over the past decade range from global deregulation, technological changes and new trends towards the international trade of services to new social developments, such as the feminization of work, remote work and part-time work. Among these, the adoption of new information technologies and working methods have been by far the most important elements with respect to changing jobs, skills and careers. A number of authors have even gone as far as to consider technology as the sole determinant of service sector employment and work organization changes (Rajam 1987, Faulhaber et al. 1986, and Japanese Service Sector report to OECD/CERI 1987).

Until the late sixties, the scale of technical progress had been rather limited, with most operations in the service sector relying on unskilled or semi-skilled personnel to perform a wide range of information-based functions. The increasing application of information technology and a changing product mix of services have led to rather dramatic changes in organizational structures, working methods, and skill requirements.

Information technology typically automates the four familiar office operations which have traditionally required human labour: organization, processing, storage and retrieval of information. For the first time in history, the service sector has been able to incorporate technical progress in its production function and, as such, has developed enormous potential to shed labour and increase future productivity. The process is a dynamic one involving varying technologies, user groups, work locations, and functions during seven progressive phases of technological application. These range from the installation of a stand-alone computer at the head office (performing mostly large scale computing operations such as payroll and accounting) to the paperless "Office of the Future" in which technology is focused on completely automating paperwork within the office (Rajam p.16).

However, not all services are becoming standardized and able to rely on mass production methods capable of scale economies and rising productivity. Hence, one should abstain from speaking of average rates of technological diffusion, average worker skills, or average organizational structures in service sectors. Major applications of information technologies in the service sector involve office automation, changes in the telecommunication system, computerization of part or all of the customer sales and service functions, electronic transfer of funds, and the computerization of design, engineering and project management functions (Ontario Task Force on Employment and New Technology 1985, pp. 102, 103).

In the absence of thorough national service industry data on stocks and flows of technology (the ECC study on Innovation and Jobs only covered a small portion of service sector industries), generalizations must rest on survey results contained in the two Ontario task forces on employment and technology in the service sector and on international material. The first noteworthy observation, at least as far as Ontario is concerned, is the slightly higher aggregate response rate of firms in the service sector in contrast to the manufacturing sector (30 percent vs. 27 percent) who reported plans to adopt new technologies prior to 1985. The response rate was an average calculated across all possible information technologies and as such may hide considerable variations. For example, the response rate of firms was 95 percent for word processing but zero for the construction of on-line terminals for group insurance customers or for the use of "smart cards," and it was only 3 percent for the introduction of fibre optics (Ontario Task Force on Employment and Technology 1985, pp. 102, 103).

The same industry survey shows a heavier use and diffusion of telecommunication and office automation technologies relative to customer sales and service technologies (Ontario Task Force On Employment and Technology 1985, pp. 106, 107). Both the ECC study on Innovation and Jobs (ECC 1987, p. 14) and the Ontario Employment and Technology and Service Sector study come up with similar rankings of service sector industries falling into high, medium, and low technology categories. Finance, insurance and real estate, and communications are typically ranked as "high tech" industries; transportation and storage, and business services as "medium tech"; and trade, amusement and recreation, food and accommodation, and other personal services are considered low technology industries. Ranking is rendered difficult for some service industries because of large intra- and inter-industry variations. This is particularly true for the business services sector which encompasses such extremes as the computer industry at one end and security and investigation services at the other end of the technology intensity continuum. It is also populated by both large multi-national corporations and one person companies.

What are the typical organizational design, human resource patterns, and consequences following the introduction of information technology in service sector industries? Foreign experience teaches us that new technologies have invariably led to decentralization processes both with respect to hierarchies in work organization and inter-branch or inter-company activities in addition to and beyond the increased deconcentration potential within economic activities (Scholz and Lippe 1987, p. 21; Bonamy 1986, p. 23; Rajam 1986, pp. 14-24; and Hirschhorn 1987, pp. 66-76). They have also led to a changed mix of "contracting out" as well as "contracting in" service functions (Hirschhorn 1987, pp. 64-76; and Andersson et al. 1987, p. 3). As a result of these developments in organizational design, work patterns have changed greatly, resulting in a tendency toward "professionalization." Translated in terms of skill formation, this has been interpreted as implying that workers would need added abilities to interact in a complex interpersonal space and would have to think more comprehensively and strategically in dynamic settings. For example, Rajam (1987, p. 225) and Hirschhorn (1987, pp. 64-76) specify four kinds of critical skills: (1) social skills for effective inter-personal communication; (2) product knowledge for effective marketing and selling of mainstream as well as ancillary services; (3) keyboard and diagnostic skills for an effective interface with systems and solving problems that arise in their use; and (4) entrepreneurial skills to ensure the viability of individual cost and profit centres. This need for new and multiple skills and their varied use in novel forms of organizational structures is equally stressed in the literature dealing with the management of service sector industries (Mills 1986).

Changes in Occupational Employment

Based on in-depth case studies in seven different British service industries, the following postulates and forecasts with respect to occupational and skill structures are provided:

> Four occupations are likely to increase their shares: professional, hybrid managerial-professional, requiring multiple competencies, clerical and sales and those providing personal services such as waiters, waitresses, cooks, etc. Use of technology and the rising knowledge and planning content of work will assist the first two groups, where most of the growth in part-time work is also expected to be concentrated. Occupations whose shares are likely to decline include branch or store based managers and operatives. An emphasis on larger but fewer outlets will reduce the need for the former and technology will reduce that of the latter (Rajam 1987, p. 7).

To get some indication of these qualitative changes as they relate to the Canadian labour force employed in the service sector, empirical evidence on changes in occupational employment and educational attainment among service industry workers from the 1971 and 1981 censuses was consulted. In addition, results from employment change decomposition analyses, also using census data (Postner and Wesa 1987), will be included.

Tables 23 and 24 show the intercensal growth in occupational employment for managerial, professional, clerical, sales and other groups for 21 service sector industries and the five service sector divisions in contrast to the overall pattern in the economy and in manufacturing. The following general observations emerge from this data.

The proportion of administrative, professional, and technical (APT) categories increased both in absolute and relative terms throughout the service sector. This could be interpreted as a reflection of the aforementioned innovations in information technology, whereby clerical workers by 1981 had more information know-how to work with as the ratio of APT per clerical worker must obviously have risen (Gershuny and Miles 1983, p. 60). However, it could also result from a volume effect in that the growth of ser-

Table 23

Employment Growth per Broad Occupational Category and Service Industries in Percentages, 1971–1981

Industry	Managerial	Professional	Clerical	Sales	Other
Manufacturing Industries	140.60	46.90	23.10	-13.30	24.20
Transport, Communications and Other Utilities	167.00	76.90	43.60	31.70	42.00
Transportation	186.80	49.40	45.90	16.50	21.90
Storage	476.60	140.00	55.80	8.80	17.90
Communications	127.00	84.10	39.60	101.20	90.30
Electric Power, Gas and Water Utilities	169.50	95.70	53.50	-15.10	-1.10
Trade	429.00	97.50	80.50	34.40	48.80
Wholesale Trade	249.70	106.90	64.70	36.50	77.70
Retail Trade	679.70	93.50	89.30	33.90	45.70
Finance, Insurance and Real Estate	154.60	126.50	72.50	63.20	487.00
Finance Industries	122.30	108.70	82.00	6.10	-1.80
Insurance Carriers	292.70	144.90	34.90	18.70	15.70
Insurance Agencies and Real Estate Industry	232.10	144.10	80.10	108.00	68.00
Community, Business and Personal Service Industries	163.30	63.70	90.30	48.70	65.40
Education and Related Services	37.50	41.50	42.20	0.30	32.40
Health and Welfare Services	163.10	70.90	84.50	24.20	61.10
Religious Organizations	54.60	59.40	60.20	56.40	13.50
Amusement and Recreation Services	220.80	101.10	113.60	54.30	101.40
Services to Business Management	166.80	148.30	121.50	105.30	115.70
Personal Services	262.10	89.10	51.80	-10.90	3.20
Accommodation and Food Services	1,608.40	76.90	143.70	29.00	91.10
Miscellaneous Services	196.20	197.40	112.60	87.60	114.90
Public Administration and Defence	104.70	63.60	52.70	-25.40	24.30
Federal Administration	76.80	31.90	37.10	-46.90	3.00
Provincial Administration	143.20	82.50	74.00	-18.90	47.30
Local Administration	131.50	98.90	66.80	12.70	62.80
Economy Total	157.90	64.20	63.20	30.30	52.60

Source: Canada Census, 1971 and 1981.

Table 24
Occupational Employment in Select Service Sector Industries in Percentages, 1971 and 1981

Industry	Managerial		Professional		Clerical		Sales		All Others	
	1971	1981	1971	1981	1971	1981	1971	1981	1971	1981
Manufacturing (Total)	12.8	22.9	13.6	14.9	42.9	39.4	20.5	13.3	10.2	9.5
Transport, Communications and Other Utilities	9.4	15.8	10.7	11.9	63.2	57.4	3.8	3.1	12.9	11.8
Transportation	9.4	17.5	9.4	9.1	56.8	54.1	5.2	3.9	19.2	15.4
Storage	12.9	36.3	2.1	2.5	66.7	51.0	10.4	5.6	7.9	4.6
Communications	8.9	12.9	6.7	7.8	73.2	65.4	2.0	2.6	9.2	11.3
Electric Power, Gas and Water Utilities	10.5	16.6	29.5	33.8	47.4	42.6	4.3	2.2	8.3	4.8
Trade	4.2	13.3	1.9	2.3	28.9	31.4	60.2	48.7	4.8	4.3
Wholesale Trade	9.7	19.8	2.3	2.8	40.7	39.2	45.5	36.3	1.8	1.9
Retail Trade	2.3	11.1	1.8	2.1	24.9	28.7	65.2	53.1	5.8	5.0
Finance, Insurance and Real Estate	13.8	19.4	2.1	2.7	53.4	50.8	24.4	22.0	6.3	5.1
Finance Industries	20.2	24.7	2.1	2.4	66.6	66.6	8.2	4.8	2.9	1.5
Insurance Carriers	6.6	17.3	3.4	5.5	51.3	46.5	36.5	29.0	2.2	1.7
Insurance Agencies and Real Estate Industry	7.1	11.7	1.3	1.6	30.5	27.1	45.5	46.7	15.6	12.9
Community, Business and Personal Service Industries	5.2	7.8	41.2	39.0	15.1	16.6	1.9	1.6	36.6	35.0
Education and Related Services	6.7	6.5	68.5	69.2	13.3	13.5	0.3	0.2	11.2	10.6
Health and Welfare Services	2.4	3.6	64.0	63.3	14.5	15.4	0.3	0.2	18.8	17.5
Religious Organizations	2.6	2.8	54.0	58.8	14.5	15.7	0.6	0.7	28.3	22.0
Amusement and Recreation Services	5.9	9.1	5.9	5.7	17.4	18.0	7.3	5.4	63.5	61.8
Services to Business Management	16.8	19.0	29.6	31.2	37.8	35.5	3.5	3.0	12.3	11.3
Personal Services	0.7	2.5	0.8	1.3	4.5	6.4	4.0	3.3	90.0	86.5
Accommodations and Food Services	0.8	7.0	0.7	0.6	7.9	9.3	2.7	1.7	87.9	81.4
Miscellaneous Services	10.8	14.1	7.6	10.0	23.4	21.9	7.3	6.0	50.9	48.0
Public Administration and Defence	13.2	18.0	15.5	16.9	33.8	34.4	0.7	0.4	36.8	30.3
Federal Administration	13.2	18.4	12.0	12.5	33.3	35.8	0.5	0.2	41.0	33.1
Provincial Administration	15.1	20.3	25.0	25.2	41.0	39.5	1.2	0.5	17.7	14.5
Local Administration	10.6	13.9	12.9	14.6	25.5	24.2	0.6	0.4	50.4	46.9
All Industries	8.1	12.6	21.9	22.1	29.7	29.9	17.6	14.1	22.7	21.3

Source: Canada Census, 1971 and 1981.

vices required the establishment of multi-office branch operations which may have led to a proliferation of managerial functions. Indeed, we note a much faster growth of management in contrast to the professional category for most service sector industries. Since information technologies are expected to reduce layers of management, the 1971 to 1981 data may merely portray the beginning or first stage of the service sector expansion with efficiency-increasing reductions in managerial personnel likely to occur during the later stages of growth. We cannot rule out entirely the possibility of the existence of organizational slack in terms of excessive management.

In order to evaluate professionalization trends in connection with the introduction of information technology, much finer occupational breakdowns would be required. Furthermore, we are likely to misinterpret some of the data because of problems with intercensal changes in occupational titles. Ideally, one would want to trace changes in information software skills. This cannot be obtained from existing data. On a broader scale, both high levels of and large growth rates in professional employment in the category of community, personal and business services (particularly business services) can be noted, and surprisingly low levels of and low growth rates in the finance, insurance and real estate sector, which had been classified earlier as "high technology." On the other hand, there is less surprise about the low level of and growth rate in professional employment in the low technology sectors such as trade, personal, and food and accommodation services. A possible explanation for the former result may be much stronger "contracting out" of services in the financial sectors of the economy analogous to what has happened in the manufacturing sector.

Sales occupations which generally grew less than the APT category showed spectacular gains only in some financial industries (e.g., insurance) and in communications.

Another way of analysing census employment data with a view to quantifying the sources of employment change is via decomposition analysis. Table 25 reproduces changes in both male and female occupational employment for select service industry related occupations, as reported in Postner and Wesa (1987, pp. 80-83). As was shown previously, columns 13 and 14 are identical for both males and females as they measure the impact of economic growth upon output and employment. Columns 12 and 11 record that part of the employment change which has been due to shifts in the composition of final demand. Columns 7 through 10 indicate employment changes due to productivity shifts (direct labour coefficients) and structural changes as measured by variations in intermediate demand. Columns 5 and 6 show an additional aspect of structural change caused by changes in occupational staffing patterns as a consequence of changes in production methods. Finally, columns 3 and 4 show employment effects associated with changes in the male/female employment mix for given occupational employment.

Table 25

Decomposition Analysis of Changes in Male and Female Occupational Employment, 1971–1981

(Selected Occupations)

Occupation	Change in Employment 1971–1981		Change of Employment Due to Change in											
			Male/Female Mix		Occupational Staffing Pattern		Direct Labour Coefficient		Input/Output Coefficient		Pattern of Final Demand		Level of Final Demand	
	Male	Female	Male	Female	Male	Female	Male	Female	Male	Female	Male	Female	Male	Female
	(1)	(2)	(3)	(4)	(5)	(6)	(7)	(8)	(9)	(10)	(11)	(12)	(13)	(14)
Systems Analysts and Computer Programmers	54.7	147.7	-18.9	72.3	37.1	36.3	-17.8	-16.2	11.2	11.7	4.1	4.4	39.1	39.1
Teaching Occupations	54.3	48.7	-2.0	1.6	13.7	4.1	-12.2	-10.2	6.0	3.2	9.7	10.9	39.1	39.1
Artistic, Recreational and Religion	49.6	108.4	-19.7	40.5	21.6	21.6	-17.1	-14.6	15.4	14.5	10.3	7.2	39.1	39.1
Health Diagnostician and Other Medical Practices	25.0	102.6	-19.3	61.5	11.5	4.3	-3.3	-0.3	-1.4	-0.5	-1.5	-1.4	39.1	39.1
Nurses, Physiotherapists and Health Technicians	49.8	68.7	-26.8	8.6	47.6	20.2	-10.9	-10.3	-2.0	3.3	2.9	7.7	39.1	39.1
Other Middle Managers	99.1	66.3	3.7	-10.2	68.4	35.2	-13.7	-9.3	4.4	8.8	-2.8	2.8	39.1	39.1
Accountants and Auditors	11.8	95.1	-19.6	71.7	-14.5	-22.4	-14.5	-11.8	17.2	14.4	4.1	4.3	39.1	39.1
Supervisors of Clerical	-29.5	54.7	-28.0	42.4	-33.8	-28.7	-16.7	-12.9	7.1	10.5	2.9	4.3	39.1	39.1
Secretaries and Stenographers	-60.2	36.3	-101.9	1.5	-8.8	-8.7	-13.8	-14.0	20.5	14.8	4.7	3.6	39.1	39.1
Bookkeepers and Accounting Clerks	2.2	81.0	-58.9	18.1	26.6	27.2	-11.6	-9.7	6.5	5.8	0.5	0.4	39.1	39.1

Table 25—Continued

Occupation	Change in Employment 1971–1981		Male/Female Mix		Change of Employment Due to Change in									
					Occupational Staffing Pattern		Direct Labour Coefficient		Input/Output Coefficient		Pattern of Final Demand		Level of Final Demand	
	Male	Female	Male	Female	Male	Female	Male	Female	Male	Female	Male	Female	Male	Female
	(1)	(2)	(3)	(4)	(5)	(6)	(7)	(8)	(9)	(10)	(11)	(12)	(13)	(14)
Tellers and Cashiers	61.1	73.9	-10.3	0.8	30.3	30.6	0.4	1.5	1.1	1.6	0.5	0.3	39.1	39.1
Telephone Operators	47.7	5.0	40.1	-1.3	-38.3	-35.8	-31.1	-32.7	19.7	21.6	12.3	14.1	39.1	39.1
Sales Occ. Services	34.1	134.6	-24.9	74.9	10.9	12.4	-8.9	-8.5	11.2	10.7	6.7	6.5	39.1	39.1
Supervisors of Service Occ.	47.6	79.1	-11.8	19.1	6.7	7.4	10.6	9.6	2.2	2.5	0.9	1.6	39.1	39.1
Protective Services	28.1	132.0	-10.4	91.8	-13.0	-11.5	-17.0	-9.8	24.6	17.1	4.9	5.3	39.1	39.1
Chefs, Cooks, and Waiters	48.3	62.0	-9.4	4.4	5.0	5.2	8.7	9.5	3.1	2.1	1.8	1.8	39.1	39.1
Lodging Services	28.8	44.9	0.6	-0.2	-17.9	-8.5	5.1	11.3	1.3	1.9	0.6	1.5	39.1	39.1
Barbers, Personal Services	12.4	39.6	-18.4	8.7	-23.3	-23.5	19.5	19.0	-1.8	-0.8	-2.6	-3.0	39.1	39.1
Janitors	23.7	66.9	-10.6	18.7	-5.5	-0.8	-0.4	7.3	1.2	2.3	-2.0	0.4	39.1	39.1
Other Service Occ.	53.6	41.2	6.7	-12.4	0.8	2.5	4.1	8.9	2.3	2.0	0.7	1.2	39.1	39.1
Truck Drivers	19.6	105.1	-1.3	76.8	-3.7	-2.5	-11.5	-8.7	0.2	2.6	-3.1	-2.1	39.1	39.1
Bus Drivers	30.4	130.2	-17.8	84.4	25.9	24.2	-16.2	-16.6	1.6	1.4	-2.2	-2.3	39.1	39.1
Total	19.2	52.3	-7.4	15.8	-0.4	0.9	-11.3	-7.4	1.5	3.8	-2.2	0.0	39.1	39.1

Source: Postner and Wesa, pp. 80–83.

The data reveals both interesting similarities and differences in male and female sources of occupational employment change. Overall, women appear to be similarly affected by changed methods of production and productivity shifts (columns 9-10 and 7-8) as well as by final demand changes (columns 11-14). Female employment as a whole, however, was subject to lower productivity gains (and hence less employment displacement) than total male employment because it was more heavily weighted by those occupations found in industries with low or stagnant productivity growth (see last row, columns 7 and 8 in table 25).

Notable differences can be found in employment effects stemming from variations in occupational staffing patterns and changes in the mix of male/female employment. Although male and female occupational employment tend to grow together, their differential growth rates (columns 1 and 2) appear to stem almost exclusively from the differential impact of the male/female mix decomposition factor (columns 3 and 4). On the other hand, changes in the occupational staffing pattern due to the intercensal shifts in the relative weight of particular industries, while accounting for some of the male/female differences, was far less important (columns 5 and 6).

From a very broad perspective, the data suggest some equalibrating of male and female employment growth in female dominated occupations (e.g., telephone operators, tellers, or other service occupations) and strong female employment growth in typically male dominated occupations (e.g., truck and bus drivers, protective services, sales, health, and artistic occupations).

Changes in Educational Attainment

Another manifestation of the trend toward professionalization has been the changing level of educational attainment among Canadian service sector workers. As can be seen from intra-sector comparisons within the service industry and comparisons with the total manufacturing sector in table 26, changes were most dramatic with respect to the decline in the stock of employed workers with less than nine years of schooling. This ratio was halved in virtually every service sector and industry, while at the same time the proportion of those with post-secondary schooling doubled over the 1971 to 1981 period.[1] These changes were much more dramatic in the service sector than in manufacturing. At face value this could be due to a slower rate of technological diffusion in manufacturing, a slower adjustment of manpower skills in this sector or both.[2] When measured in terms of increases in average educational attainment, this trend was strongest for the health and public administration sector, followed by business services and the financial sector (in that order).

Table 26

Educational Attainment among Workers in Service Sector Industries, 1971 and 1981

1971

Industry	Less than 9 Years	9–11 Years	12–13 Years	Total Secondary	Some University	University Degree	Total Tertiary
Manufacturing Industries	33.80	36.60	19.90	56.50	6.20	3.60	9.80
Transport, Communications and Other Utilities	27.80	38.75	22.95	61.70	7.06	3.43	10.49
Transportation	35.72	38.69	17.34	56.03	60.80	2.17	62.97
Storage	30.92	41.20	20.40	61.60	5.49	1.99	7.48
Communications	10.78	41.02	34.43	75.45	9.23	4.53	13.76
Electric Power, Gas and Water Utilities	22.48	34.35	27.87	62.22	7.83	7.47	15.30
Trade	22.02	42.84	25.37	68.21	7.16	2.62	9.78
Wholesale Trade	21.61	38.96	27.25	66.21	8.50	3.68	12.18
Retail Trade	22.17	44.30	24.66	68.96	6.65	2.22	8.87
Finance, Insurance and Real Estate	8.35	31.98	41.97	73.95	11.54	6.16	17.70
Finance Industries	5.59	31.49	45.81	77.30	11.31	5.80	17.11
Insurance Carriers	5.50	31.09	43.36	74.45	12.06	7.99	20.05
Insurance Agencies and Real Estate Industry	15.34	33.51	34.02	67.53	11.57	5.56	17.13
Community, Bus. and Personal Service Industries	18.72	28.38	24.15	52.53	12.05	16.71	28.76
Education and Related Services	8.12	14.33	22.43	36.76	20.46	34.66	55.12
Health and Welfare Services	15.83	30.77	30.81	61.58	9.97	12.63	22.60
Religious Organizations	22.09	22.05	15.62	37.67	10.30	29.94	40.24
Amusement and Recreation Services	21.20	35.48	26.32	61.80	12.41	4.59	17.00
Services to Business Management	8.26	24.19	31.94	56.13	12.28	23.29	35.57
Personal Services	35.73	45.39	14.44	59.83	3.61	0.83	4.44
Accommodation and Food Services	34.48	39.16	18.14	57.30	6.67	1.56	8.23
Miscellaneous Services	27.97	35.21	23.21	58.42	8.39	5.22	13.61
Public Administration and Defence	15.90	35.35	27.15	62.50	10.85	10.75	21.60
Federal Administration	12.91	37.92	26.88	64.80	10.65	11.66	22.31
Provincial Administration	13.18	29.95	29.91	59.86	12.67	14.29	26.96
Local Administration	25.54	35.50	24.82	60.32	9.29	4.84	14.13
Other Government Offices	20.26	36.42	22.20	58.62	12.07	9.05	21.12

Table 26—Continued

1981

Industry	Less than 9 Years	9–13 Years No Diploma	9–13 Years Diploma	Trade Certificate	Total Secondary	Some University	University Degree	Total Tertiary
Manufacturing Industries	20.11	28.80	15.20	14.80	58.80	11.30	9.90	21.20
Transport, Communications and Other Utilities	13.84	27.19	17.11	14.69	58.99	14.36	12.81	27.17
Transportation	18.38	30.28	14.50	14.58	59.36	12.40	9.86	22.26
Storage	15.08	38.41	17.15	9.79	65.35	12.47	7.11	19.58
Communications	5.18	23.66	24.12	10.90	58.68	18.85	17.29	36.14
Electric Power, Gas and Water Utilities	10.43	18.26	14.97	23.51	56.74	14.60	18.23	32.83
Trade	10.89	32.68	18.89	12.59	64.16	14.08	10.89	24.97
Wholesale Trade	11.16	28.73	18.66	13.14	60.53	15.54	12.78	28.32
Retail Trade	10.79	34.79	18.98	12.90	66.67	13.51	9.04	22.55
Finance, Insurance and Real Estate	4.33	19.83	26.51	10.05	56.39	19.56	19.72	39.28
Finance Industries	2.34	20.16	31.58	7.86	59.60	20.39	17.67	38.06
Insurance Carriers	2.84	17.01	28.49	10.51	56.01	19.81	21.34	41.15
Insurance Agencies and Real Estate Industry	8.22	20.69	17.49	13.28	51.46	18.13	12.18	40.31
Community, Bus. and Personal Service Industries	12.41	24.64	13.41	12.07	50.12	13.97	23.49	37.46
Education and Related Services	9.84	15.01	12.21	10.23	37.45	15.55	37.16	52.71
Health and Welfare Services	10.37	16.91	10.44	13.66	41.01	10.98	37.65	48.63
Religious Organizations	20.73	19.88	12.09	9.09	41.06	12.97	25.25	38.22
Amusement and Recreation Services	10.17	31.90	16.41	8.11	56.42	20.02	13.39	33.41
Services to Business Management	5.21	18.30	17.53	11.03	46.86	20.56	27.37	47.83
Personal Services	17.85	26.91	10.87	28.72	66.50	8.32	7.33	15.65
Accommodation and Food Services	17.10	40.04	15.38	7.41	62.83	13.08	6.99	20.07
Miscellaneous Services	16.28	27.15	13.75	14.47	55.37	14.66	13.69	28.35
Public Administration and Defence	8.52	19.93	18.23	14.22	52.38	17.59	21.51	39.10
Federal Administration	5.85	21.24	19.10	15.66	56.00	18.13	20.02	38.15
Provincial Administration	6.28	16.04	19.69	12.92	48.65	18.21	26.86	45.07
Local Administration	14.56	21.69	15.54	13.35	50.58	16.19	18.66	34.85
Other Government Offices	8.55	17.47	20.45	10.41	48.33	20.45	22.68	43.13

Source: Canada Census, 1971 and 1981.

Note: The category "trade certificate" in the 1981 data includes workers with training in community colleges, special vocational institutes, private business colleges, etc. They are not shown separately in the 1971 data, but are instead distributed within the secondary education classification.

A number of authors have advanced the hypothesis that there has been a polarization of skills in services and that this in turn would lead to a number of consequences with respect to human resource development and the distribution of earnings (Berger and Piore 1980, Tolbert et al. 1980). Skills cannot be measured *per se,* but to the extent that education or years of schooling can be used as a close proxy we can examine skill polarization in terms of the distribution of educational attainment among workers in different service sector industries. Skill polarization could be defined as the simultaneous existence of both low and high levels of educational attainment among workers in given service sector industries. Looking at table 26, we find a redistribution of workers between 1971 and 1981 away from the category of those with less than nine years of schooling and toward categories of higher educational attainment, notably post-secondary. Only in the case of transportation, storage, retail trade, accommodation and food, personal and miscellaneous service do we observe employment patterns containing a large share of both highly unskilled and skilled workers. These industries fall mainly into the low productivity and low technology category.

It is well beyond the scope of this investigation to pursue a causal model or explanation of the differential pattern of technology diffusion, productivity, and human resource development across all service sector industries. We only note that skill polarization, at least when measured in terms of educational attainment, appears to be neither a common characteristic nor a common trend among service sector industries. If anything, we observe a general rise in educational attainment throughout most of the service sector.

This change in educational attainment also highlights the problem of less skilled workers. According to economy-wide decomposition calculations provided by Postner and Wesa (1987, p. 111) using three educational attainment groups—less than nine years of schooling, some high school, and some university—the least educated are particularly vulnerable to structural change and to the changing educational mix in the economy. While the group with some university education increased its employment level in the business sector by 67 percent from 1971 to 1981 and the group with some high school education showed gains of 42 percent, the least educated lost over 33 percent in employment.

There have been profound changes in the underlying structure or production function of a number of service sector industries brought on by increased competition, shorter innovation cycles, higher quality requirements, and the introduction of new information technologies. This seems to have led to transformations of employment systems and changes in work organization, both of which were conditioned by varying rates of technology diffusion and socio-cultural work-force characteristics among regions, industries, and countries. As computer systems move from the fringes of the production process to the centre and provide integrated automation, they no longer affect specific functions and occupations such as processing clerks, back office employees, typists, secretaries, inventory control personnel, engineers, or draftsmen but impact on almost everybody in the organization in terms of increased requirements of computer literacy.[3] If anything, the speed of these changes seems to have hastened during the eighties (Fossum 1983, Ianrif 1984, ECC 1987). It follows that the transformation in and growth of the service sector must have required quantitative and qualitative changes in the supply of skilled workers. This, in turn, poses questions as to the adequacy of the response of the Canadian systems of education and training.

Service Sector Skills and Canadian Systems of Education and Training

It is impossible to provide a thorough and systematic evaluation of the adequacy of the response of Canadian education and training to either short- or long-term changes in the demand for specific skills. Apart from statistical problems due to changes in the categorization of fields of study and inter- and intra-provincial quality variations, there is the even greater hurdle of connecting education (and to a lesser extent training) to specific occupations and skills. Notwithstanding these difficulties, an attempt is made below to relate changes in Canadian education and training during the seventies to the expansion of the service sector over the same period of time. We are helped in this particular decade by the prevalence of numerous task forces, research reports, and evaluation programmes associated with labour market behaviour and designing training policies (ECC 1982, Maki 1978, Employment and Immigration Canada 1977, 1981).

While basic statistics on enrolment in education and training are available for the 1980s, there has been less research directed at specific sectors, occupations, industries or labour market segments for this period. The emphasis has been on the overall functioning of the economy and the adjustment of labour. Nowhere has this lack of empirical work and specificity been more obvious than in the various research reports on labour market aspects underlying the Royal Commission Report on the Economic Union and Development Prospects for Canada (Riddell et al. 1986). Our interpretations should therefore be treated cautiously in recognition of apparent gaps in both data and relevant research findings.

Tables 27 and 28 give some idea of the changing distribution of student enrolment by broad fields of study. In table 29, we replicate labour market experience data of university and college graduates reported by Statistics Canada (1981). Tables 30, 31, and 32 show the distribution of trainees in federal manpower training programmes across industry and occupation and compare them with overall labour market data.

Table 27

**Percentage Distribution of Full-Time Undergraduates by Discipline in Canada,
1960–1986**

	1960	1970	1977	1986
Arts, Science and Education	64.1	73.0	67.0	66.0
Engineering	15.0	9.3	10.4	10.0
Medical and Health	9.0	6.3	6.9	6.0
Business and Commerce	6.1	6.1	10.0	12.1
Law	2.3	2.6	3.0	2.5
Other	3.6	2.7	2.7	3.4

Source: *Employment and Immigration Canada: Labour Market Developments in the 1980s*,
p. 156, and own calculations for 1986.

Table 28

**Percentage Share of Enrolment in Canadian Community Colleges by Broad Field of
Specialization, 1970–1985**

Specialization	1970/71		1974/75	1985/86
Applied Arts		10.8	12.1	8.8
Business and Commerce		31.2	25.9	29.0
Technological Fields (Total)		24.0	18.2	28.5
Chemical	3.4		2.1	1.4
Electrical and Electronic	9.1		6.1	15.1
Engineering	11.5		10.0	12.0
National Resource and		4.8	4.3	4.5
Primary Industries				
Medical Fields		11.8	24.8	14.8
Social and Community Services		6.0	11.3	13.8
Other Technologies n.e.r.		11.4	3.4	0.6
Total	100.0	100.0	100.0	

Source: Statistics Canada, *Education in Canada*, catalogue 81-229, and Statistics Canada,
Community Colleges and Related Institutions 1970/71, catalogue 81-222.

Judging from the labour force experience data among university and college graduates, groups with the lowest levels of unemployment and underemployment were university graduates in business and commerce, education, engineering, architecture, dentistry, and pharmacy, which comprise more or less the traditional professions. For college graduates, they include data processing, medical and dental services, and various technologies (tables 27-32, Employment and Immigration 1980, p. 155; ECC 1982, pp. 91, 92). This appears to support the earlier reported trend toward professionalization of work in the setting of the service sector. There is evidence that similar developments are under way in the manufacturing sector as well (see ECC 1987).

Table 29

Labour Force Experience for 1976

University Graduates by Field of Study, Canada,[1] June 1978

Field of Study	Number of Graduates	Unemployment Rate	Employed in Unrelated Work	Under-Employed
Business, Management and Commerce	5,030	4.4	8.9	27.6
Education	12,796	4.6	11.7	26.8
Fine and Applied Arts	2,115	14.3	20.0	38.5
Humanities	10,888	10.8	28.2	45.9
Social Sciences	17,479	10.0	26.3	42.7
Agriculture and Biology	5,443	11.0	25.3	37.5
Engineering and Applied Science	3,573	4.4	7.4	13.8
Health	3,226	4.4	2.7	18.8
Mathematics and Physical Science	4,274	9.7	18.1	29.8
General	759	8.5	24.3	46.8
All Graduates	66,481	8.2	18.8	34.3

Note: [1] without Quebec.

Source: Economic Council of Canada, *In Short Supply: Jobs and Skills in the 1980s*, p. 91.

Table 30

Distribution of AOTA Trainees in 1974/75 and Longer Term Vacancies (1974) by Occupation

	CCDO Occupation	CMTP Skill Training	CMITP	Total	Long-Term Vacancies
21	Natural Science, Engineering and Mathematics	1.6	3.2	2.1	9.1
31	Medicine and Health	4.4	2.5	3.7	6.4
41	Clerical and Related	24.8	6.9	18.8	9.1
51	Sales	1.4	5.7	2.9	7.4
61	Service	6.6	5.7	6.3	11.6
71	Farming and Horticulture	15.6	0.9	10.6	0.0
73	Fishing and Hunting	2.0	0.1	1.4	0.0
75	Forestry and Logging	1.9	2.3	2.0	0.0
81/2	Processing	1.8	13.9	5.9	4.7
83	Machining and Related	8.1	12.6	9.6	8.9
85	Project Fabrication and Assembly	13.9	25.9	17.9	17.9
87	Construction	8.2	6.1	7.5	6.9
91	Transport Equipment Operator	5.1	2.0	4.1	3.4
	All Other	4.6	12.2	7.2	14.6
	Total	100.0	100.0	100.0	100.0

Source: D. Maki, 1978, p. 107.

Table 31

Distribution of Employment, Job Vacancies and AOTA Trainees by Occupation, Canada, 1977–1980

Occupation	Employment 1979	Job Vacancies 1977–79	AOTA Trainees 1979/80	
			CMTP	CMITP
Managerial and Professional	22.9	16.8	10.5	9.1
Clerical	17.1	5.4	24.7	8.5
Sales	10.4	6.0	1.4	6.6
Service	12.9	7.6	9.7	6.1
Primary	6.4	8.8	6.6	5.5
Processing	15.8	42.1	28.1	44.2
Construction Trades	6.4	8.0	10.1	6.3
Other Trades and Crafts	8.1	5.2	8.9	13.7
Total	100.0	100.0	100.0	100.0

Source: Economic Council of Canada, *In Short Supply: Jobs and Skills in the 1980s*, p. 85.

Table 32

Distribution of Employment, Unemployment and General Industrial Training and Critical Skills Training by Industry Groups, 1984/85

Industry SIC Group	Employment 1984	Unemployment 1984	General Industrial Training	Critical Skill Training
Agriculture	3.5	2.3	1.9	0.3
Fishing	0.3	0.5	0.3	0.3
Forestry	0.5	2.2	1.4	0.7
Mines, Quarries and Oil Wells	1.7	1.8	3.0	3.2
Manufacturing (Total)	18.0	17.7	36.9	53.1
Construction	4.9	13.2	5.4	4.9
Transportation, Communication and Other Utilities	8.0	5.7	3.0	6.1
Trade	17.7	15.6	16.0	7.7
Finance, Insurance and Real Estate	5.7	2.5	0.6	0.2
Community, Business and Personal Service	32.6	25.3	16.7	12.2
Public Administration	7.1	5.4	3.3	0.9
Unspecified	—	5.6	11.5	10.4
Total	100.0	100.0	100.0	100.0

Source: Employment and Immigration, Annual Statistics Bulletin, National Training Program 1984/85, Statistics Canada, April 1984, The Labour Force, catalogue 71-001.

To what extent has the Canadian education and training system adjusted to these longer term trends? While education and training data should be interpreted with considerable caution, the overall impression is one of considerable institutional inertia and adjustment lag. For example, in professional education only, business studies increased its share from 6 percent in 1960 to 12.1 percent in 1986, engineering and health, on the other hand, lowered their share over the same period of time. Arts, science, and education had a large buildup by the early seventies but by 1986 had fallen back to the share it had in the sixties.

The situation is somewhat, although not drastically, different in non-university post-secondary education. Community colleges, which in Canada developed only during the late sixties, were originally designed for applied fields in health, business, and technology—a pattern which, with the exception of health, is reflected in the enrolment figures for 1970/71. During the seventies, community colleges underwent a considerable period of experimentation not entirely induced by labour demand changes but which also originated from the industry's programme proliferation and grantsmanship with the help of provincial funding. By 1985/86 ratios were again close to what they were in the early seventies. Overall, community colleges appeared to have been relatively more responsive to underlying changes in the demand for qualifications. This can be seen in the expansion of technology-related fields, particularly data processing and information technology (classified under electrical and electronic), as well as in the secular increase in enrolment for the category of social and community services. While a good case can be made for "high quality general education" being the best insurance against technological change, allowing individuals a large degree of occupational flexibility, there is a minimum amount of occupational preparation and specialization required. It is questionable whether that has been forthcoming in Canada's system of education (Weiermair 1984).

Similar institutional inertia, or adjustment lags towards professionalization and new qualifications, has been carried forward in federal manpower training programmes. Through their "seat purchase" and provincial cost sharing programmes throughout the seventies, these training programmes were closely linked to developments in the formal system of education. Looking at tables 30 and 31, we see a very low correspondence between training occupations and long-term vacancies (as a rough measure of skill shortages). This has been particularly true for managerial and professional, and sales and service occupations which are all prominent in the service sector. On the other hand, there appears to have been an overexpansion of clerical training in comparison to vacancy trends.

The situation has hardly changed in the eighties as evidenced by industry data on employment, unemployment, and federally sponsored training. Relative to the distribution of employment and unemployment, training appears to have been heavily biased towards manufacturing. Again, the point could be made that proper training in service sector industries would have helped raise skill standards and thus employability in a sector which had been growing much faster. These arguments are not novel but have been made repeatedly in the past without succeeding in changing policy (Maki 1978, p. 116 ff).

The disappointing record of Canadian institutions of learning and training to adapt to long-run changes in technology and labour demand, which in the eighties has been exacerbated by declining enrolment, has deep roots in the way Canadian universities are financed and controlled. As pointed out by Leslie, "there is hardly any carrot for innovation" and only a "flimsy stick for inducing structural changes where necessary" thus preventing the "invention of solutions to staffing problems and program redundancy or overcapacity" (1980, pp. 314-315). Adjustments are particularly hard to implement in those fields which involve high levels of specialization.

Before concluding this section on structural change, we should briefly investigate possible alternative means of skill acquisition open to firms in Canadian service sector industries, notably immigration, apprenticeship, and other forms of on-the-job training and retraining. Whether Canada has obtained the requisite skill needed for the expansion of her service sector through immigration in the past and whether the skill gap opened up by lags in education and training can be covered by the import of skilled workers in the future remains very much an open question. As noted by an earlier federal task force, "obtaining the skills Canada needs in the eighties has become complicated by a relative reduction in the attractiveness of Canadian wages and working conditions relative to traditional countries of emigration and immigration" (Employment and Immigration Canada 1981, p. 187). In addition, federal control in matching immigration with foreign labour supply on the basis of calculations of Canadian shortages in particular occupational groups has been marred by a host of problems in methodology and administration as illustrated, for example, in the entrepreneur immigrant programme (Wong et al. 1985). Given the unreliability of the data, which is only based on information regarding the intended occupations of immigrants, and the problems of matching immigrant labour supply to particular skill gaps, especially those opened up by recent technological changes in a number of specific service sectors, utmost caution should be exercised in interpreting trends in immigration statistics.

Looking at table 33, we find a relative secular increase in service-related intended occupations as compared to secondary and primary sector occupations. Among broad occupational groupings, immigration in the category of professional, technical, and clerical workers has gradually lost its share. This may have been due to either ample Canadian supplies (as in the case of clerical workers), standard professional qualifications, or small foreign labour supplies (such as may have been the case with highly specialized professional and technical workers). Changes of immigration policies in the seventies which have constrained economic immigration in favour of non-economic immigration (family re-unification, political refugees, et cetera) have further contributed to widening possible mismatches between skill requirements and immigration.

Table 33

Immigration to Canada by (intended) Groups of Occupation, Selected Years

(percentage)

Occupational Group	1979	1981	1985
Managerial	7.2	6.0	8.3
Professional and Technical	23.3	27.5	22.8
Clerical	14.8	16.7	11.1
Commercial and Financial	4.6	4.2	5.3
Service and Recreation	10.5	10.8	19.3
Transport and Communication	2.1	1.2	2.1
Agriculture	4.1	3.7	3.8
Mining and Quarrying	0.4	0.5	0.7
Manufacturing	33.0	29.5	26.6

Source: *Canadian Statistical Review*, various issues.

From a very broad and long-term perspective, immigration seems to have moved in the same direction as the composition of growth in Canadian occupational and industrial demand for labour. However, little evidence is available which would confirm the extent to which foreign labour supplies have contributed to adjusting labour imbalances, particularly those created by the transformation of the service sector.

Turning to industrial and employer sponsored training programmes as a means of skill acquisition and as a source of supply for correcting quality imbalances in labour markets, we are faced with an even greater knowledge and data gap. Information is restricted to a number of occasional national or provincial surveys on training in industry (Betcherman 1982, Ontario Manpower Commission 1986, Ontario Task Force on Employment and New Technology 1985, Statistics Canada 1973). Apprenticeship, which combines institutional and industrial training, traditionally has played a smaller role in Canada than elsewhere. Its major focus has been relatively restricted to a small number of trades in the construction and metal fabricating industries. Apart from providing training in a small number of apprenticeable service sector occupations such as barbers (personal services), cooks (accommodation and food) or watch makers, car mechanics, and TV repairmen (retail trade), Canada's apprenticeship training system has been unable to expand and develop the appropriate mix of skills typical of a changing service sector (Weiermair 1984).

In terms of employer-sponsored service sector training and retraining, the following can be learned from various surveys in Ontario (Ontario

Manpower Commission 1986, Ontario Task Force on Employment and New Technology 1985).

The incidence of formal training programmes in the service sector in 1984 was about the industry average (27 percent), with the trade sector reporting 27.4 percent of their establishments, and the finance and business services, and other services reporting 27.2 and 26.9 percent of their establishments having formal training programmes (Ontario Manpower Commission 1986, p. 12).

The ranking changes slightly when training proportions are based on the percentage of employees participating in formal training (industry average 13.3 percent, trade 9.7 percent, transportation, communication, and utilities 11.3 percent, finance and business services 15.7 percent, health and education 14.8 percent, other services 8.5 percent (Ontario Manpower Commission 1986, p. 16).

There is a general inverse relationship between establishment size and the provision of formal training (below 20 employees 23.9 percent, 20-199 employees 51.1 percent, 200 and more employees 87.8 percent (Ontario Manpower Commission 1986, p. 12).

Training propensities increase with the level of education or skill as evidenced by the much higher proportions of training involvement among the managerial, administrative, professional, and technical category (Ontario Manpower Commission 1986, p. 18).

The typical response pattern of service sector organizations towards skill shortages resulting from technological change is to recruit or retrain existing personnel. About 45 percent of firms in more than 14 different service industries in Ontario would choose recruiting as their most likely step to resolving manpower shortages while another 45 percent would undertake retraining. Interestingly, relocation or contracting out was only mentioned in the insurance brokerage industry and was only cited as the third most likely step to be undertaken (Ontario Task Force on Employment and New Technology 1986, p. 70.)

To conclude, this section has shown that most Canadian service sector industries have undergone profound changes in their production function as evidenced by changes in the sector's occupational structure and workers' educational attainment. Questions were raised, however, as to whether skill formation alternatives in the form of immigration and Canadian systems of education and training were adequate for meeting changing labour quality requirements. We will address this question again in chapter 5 when discussing labour market imbalances.

Summary

The evolution of the nature and composition of jobs in the service industries over the past 20 years has, in large part, been dominated by the introduction of information technologies. While other industries have also faced changes in information systems, firms in the service sector have shown a more rapid adoption of these new technologies. Other important changes which the service sector underwent in the past 20 years include socio-economic developments which led to the increased feminization of work and an increased emphasis on part-time employment. Deregulation both at home and abroad have led to increased domestic and international competition. It has been argued that these developments caused a higher level of "professionalization" and increases in the span of control for many service sector occupations. In many service operations, new technologies have eliminated lower level tasks and have thereby increased both the responsibility and productivity of individual workers. Increases in skill levels in the service sector (approximated by educational attainment) have also been observed and can be partly attributed to the need for greater skills resulting from technological changes. It has been noted that the response of the Canadian education and training system to these changes in the service sector may have been both insufficient and slow. As a result, we have noticed increases in the mismatching of jobs and skills expressed in terms of such conventional measures as occupational unemployment and shortages or vacancies. Skill shortages also could not entirely be eradicated through immigration due to labour market developments abroad and changes in Canadian immigration laws.

NOTES

1. Note, however, the accentuation of these changes because of the differential treatment of community college education in the 1971 and 1981 censuses.

2. These results should not surprise us given the relatively higher technology intensity reported for the services sector (for some recent evidence see ECC 1987, p. 74).

3. For an excellent general discussion and case studies see OECD/CERI (1986).

Chapter 5

INDUSTRIAL RELATIONS, WAGES, AND LABOUR COST IN THE SERVICE SECTOR

Since wage and labour cost developments are closely linked to collective bargaining, for the unionized service sector at least, this section starts with a discussion of the broader industrial relations developments which have recently taken place. Included are such issues as union growth, attempts to unionize specific service sector industries, and the past treatment and settlement of today's most thorny industrial relations problems, including pay equity, part-time work, flexible working time arrangements, and introduction of new technologies at the work place.

In the second part I will discuss wage developments, wage differences between the sexes, and the question of the declining middle in the income distribution of the service sector. Some wage and labour cost comparisons and wage determination models are also presented.

Industrial Relations in the Service Sector

Tables 34 through 36 show broad unionization trends, collective agreement coverage for white collar employees by broad sector, and collective agreement coverage by service sector industry groupings. As elsewhere, Canadian union density trends have shown declines in those core industries which underwent big structural changes and downsizing (manufacturing, construction, and parts of the primary sector) while at the same time showing gains in the fast growing service sector. Challenges from legal decisions flowing from the new Charter of Rights and Freedoms and the recessionary impact of the 1981/82 downturn of economic activity have combined to reverse the secular trends in union membership which peaked in 1983. As a consequence, unions have been most anxious to organize the unorganized work-force in order to increase membership.

Table 34
Unionization Trends
(union members as a percentage of paid workers)

Industry	1972	1976	1979	1981	1983	1985
Primary	28.4	25.2	17.9	38.1	21.1	20.6
Manufacturing	43.4	43.5	40.9	44.4	41.8	37.9
Construction	65.8	52.1	43.9	54.4	62.6	47.8
Transport and Communication	51.1	50.0	48.3	53.2	59.6	53.1
Trade	7.3	8.5	7.8	8.9	9.1	9.9
Finance	1.3	2.7	2.4	2.8	2.5	2.7
Service	21.3	22.6	22.5	25.6	33.9	36.2
Public Administration	61.2	67.4	67.8	69.1	72.4	70.8
Total	32.2	32.2	30.3	32.9	35.7	34.4

Source: Statistics Canada, Corporations and Labour Unions Return Act, Part II, Labour Unions, various years.

Table 35
Collective Agreement Coverage for White Collar Employees
(percentage)

	1971	1976	1978	1981	1983	1985
All Employees*	32	40	42	43	43	43
Manufacturing	8	10	10	10	10	10
Transport, Storage, Communication and Utilities	44	43	43	44	46	50
Trade and Commerce						
Office	3	4	3	3	4	4
Sales**	32	29	31	36	15	16
Finance	2	2	2	3	3	3
Service Workers						
Office	19	25	27	30	31	33
Nurses and Technicians	56	74	73	83	83	83
Public Service	74	92	88	89	85	83

Source: Industrial Relations Centre, Queen's University, *The Current Industrial Relations Scene in Canada*, 1986.

Notes: *Includes all office employees, sales personnel, nurses and technicians.

** Surveys after 1981 excluded retail cashiers from sales and placed retail cashiers in the non-office category. Thus, figures under "Trade-Sales" after 1981 are not comparable with figures before 1982.

Table 36

Collective Agreement Coverage by Industry Group for the Service Sector Only

Industry	1971			1979			1984		
	Office	Non-Office	Other	Office	Non-Office	Other	Office	Non-Office	Other
Transportation and Communication	46	84	86	44	89	89	50	94	91
Air Transport	46	87	87	34	92	85	31	93	93
Water Transport	3	61	79	29	78	91	26	87	92
Stevedoring	17	81	–	27	97	–	26	97	–
Railway Transport	53	95	99	41	98	100	42	98	98
Truck Transport	4	67	65	9	56	72	13	61	70
Bus Transport	25	55	70	23	73	71	48	78	74
Urban Transport Systems	24	96	98	31	98	99	29	94	99
Grain Elevators	21	49	–	23	63	–	28	72	–
Radio and TV Broadcasting	26	55	–	30	66	–	56	78	–
Telephone Systems	56	98	–	50	94	–	55	98	–
Electric Power	58	88	–	59	95	–	63	94	–
Trade	3	22	32	4	26	25	5	46	17
Wholesale	3	25	–	4	34	6	4	38	7
Retail Food Stores	7	61	70	6	43	81	9	85	–
Motor Vehicle Repairs	2	20	5	1	20	6	–	15	5
Retail, Other	3	11	10	4	14	7	7	12	20
Finance	2	9	–	3	17	–	3	12	–

Table 36—Continued

Industry	1971			1979			1984		
	Office	Non-Office	Other	Office	Non-Office	Other	Office	Non-Office	Other
Service	19	37	—	29	49	—	31	52	80
Hospitals	41	65	56	49	81	76	49	82	83
Laundries, Cleaners and Pressers	4	30	—	11	35	—	2	29	
Hotels, 200 or More Employees	10	75	—	5	61	—	6	66	
Hotels, Less than 200 Employees	4	19	—	7	22	—	4	22	
Restaurants	1	13	—	1	19	—	1	17	—
Public Administration	74	84	—	90	97	97	83	88	98

Source: Labour Canada, *Working Conditions in Canadian Industry*.

Notes: 1 "Office" employees refer to supervisory, professional and technical staff, and personnel engaged in clerical, accounting, secretarial, sales, executive and administrative activities.

2 "Non-Office" employees refer to non-supervisory workers directly engaged in the production of goods or services and the provision of maintenance and auxiliary services closely associated with production operations.

3 "Other" employees include certain operating workers, sales employees, nursing and technical staff and firemen and policemen. These groups of employees are found in four industry divisions: transportation, retail trade, hospitals, and local administration.

Given the employment growth potential of the service sector and the existence of earnings and working condition differentials between manufacturing and services and within services industries, unions have begun to target service sector issues and service sector organizations. The recent drive by unions to achieve legislative change on pay, employment equity, and child care have to be viewed and understood in light of these broader developments. Unions were successful to the extent that they were able to raise membership between 1982 and 1987 in the 16 largest service-sector-related unions (Industrial Relations Centre 1987, p. 40). However, judging from annual statistics on recent certification activity, unions appear to have been less successful as both total applications processed and certifications granted show substantial declines in the 1984 to 1986 period in comparison with the earlier period of 1980 to 1983. At the same time there has been an increase in decertification (Industrial Relations Centre 1987 p. 38).

While the total rate of unionization in Canada is higher for male workers than for female workers in primary industries, the same is not true for the service sector. With the exception of transportation, storage, and utilities, service sector industries show a higher ratio of unionized female workers than unionized male workers. Furthermore, those ratios have risen faster for females than for males (Industrial relations Centre 1987 p. 375). Clearly, unions have centred their campaigns in the service sector around full- and part-time female workers, leading at times to bitter labour strife, strikes, and lockouts, particularly in cases of certification and first contract negotiation.

In many instances, low service sector wages were not the only driving force behind unionization. In the exceptional cases of banks and retail chains, the causes appear to have been arbitrary promotion practices, management training practices discriminating against women, and management mistreatment of individual employees—in short, poor management (Lowe 1981, p. 879; McGrath 1984, p. 59). Although the evidence on unionization forces may be less than conclusive, it is nevertheless fair to observe that most service sector unionization has been very closely associated with problems of female employment, notably discriminatory practices.

As is to be expected, there is a high correlation between union density and the incidence of strikes and lockouts across broader industrial groupings in select years (see table 37). For example, strikes and lockouts are much more prevalent both in terms of workers involved and man-days lost in manufacturing than in the service sector. Within the service sector, subsectors with low rates of unionization, such as trade and finance, and real estate and insurance, show a lower strike record than the more highly unionized transportation, storage and utilities, public administration, and community and business services subsectors. Beyond that, we notice a con-

Table 37

Strikes and Lockouts

Percentage Distribution by Industry

	1967	1971	1975	1979	1984
Number					
Primary	5.7	8.3	5.2	5.0	2.8
Manufacturing	51.1	48.9	44.7	48.7	47.8
Construction	22.8	12.7	10.4	4.6	5.0
Transport, Storage, Communications and Utilities	8.2	9.7	9.7	12.3	6.7
Trade	3.6	8.1	7.6	7.4	14.1
Finance	0.4	0.2	0.9	1.7	3.2
Services	5.9	7.6	14.0	13.3	15.6
Public Administration	2.1	4.8	7.4	7.0	4.7
Workers Involved					
Primary	3.5	6.8	9.2	7.5	1.7
Manufacturing	36.3	39.4	29.6	36.2	57.8
Construction	16.9	10.0	11.6	2.6	10.4
Transport, Storage, Communications and Utilities	11.8	19.1	16.5	19.3	10.7
Trade	1.2	2.0	3.9	4.0	3.1
Finance	n/a	0.1	0.5	0.5	0.3
Services	26.1	18.0	12.0	15.7	14.2
Public Administration	4.1	4.6	6.8	14.2	1.8
Person-Days Lost					
Primary	1.3	9.9	13.5	21.8	1.0
Manufacturing	49.7	53.8	48.9	40.2	60.5
Construction	24.6	14.0	9.0	1.1	5.5
Transport, Storage, Communication and Utilities	10.8	8.9	12.8	15.2	14.1
Trade	1.2	2.8	3.5	3.2	4.9
Finance	n/a	n/a	1.5	0.5	1.2
Services	9.1	7.7	6.9	9.8	10.8
Public Administration	3.3	2.9	3.7	8.3	2.0

Source: Strikes and Lockouts, in *The Current Industrial Relations Scene in Canada*, 1985.

siderable intertemporal and intra-industrial variation in strike activity, suggesting differential causes in terms of working conditions, industrial relations issues, and labour-management relations.

While it is virtually impossible to accurately depict all these variations in Canada's highly decentralized and fragmented industrial relations environment, some insights may be gained by focusing on management's and labour's varied approaches and attitudes towards major industrial relations issues in the service sector. These issues are: technological change, part-time work, and pay equity. Evidence on the industrial relations aspect of technological change in the context of Canadian service sector industries comes from the reports of the Ontario Task Force on Employment and New Technology (1985) and the Economic Council of Canada's study on Innovation and Jobs (1987). A first important finding seems to be the observation that "new technologies appear to be threatening union membership by accelerating employment shifts away from traditionally unionized occupations." There also appears to be a tendency for collective bargaining coverage to be stronger in the medium and low technology industries (ECC 1987, pp. 110-111). Keeping this aspect of collective bargaining coverage and location in mind, the social partners' disposition towards technological change can be evaluated in terms of the frequency of technological change provisions in collective agreements and in terms of the degree of and mechanism for worker participation. The following observations pertinent to the service sector emerge.

Among the various technological change provisions most frequently cited were the following (in decreasing order of importance):

- advance notice/consultation,
- contracting out prohibitions,
- training/retraining,
- employment security,
- labour management committee on technological change,
- notice of layoff resulting from technological change, and
- relocation allowance.

There are only negligible differences between service sectors and other industries (Ontario Task Force 1985, p. 78; ECC 1987, p. 114). Between 1972 and 1985, all types of technological change provisions have risen, so has the percentage of workers covered (ECC 1987, p. 115).

All five industries which showed the lowest average frequency of technological change clauses in collective agreements came from the service sector. They were: primary and secondary schools, hotels and motels, postsecondary non-university educational institutions, air transportation, and grocery stores. No service sector industries were included in the list of the five highest scoring industries.[1]

All the industries which showed the highest levels of increase in negotiated technological change provisions between 1978 and 1984 (extraction, communication and utilities, manufacturing, and public administration) were identified in previous studies (Magun 1985) as those having suffered the largest employment losses due to technological change (Knight 1985, p. 423). The results are not surprising given the strong presence of unions in those two service sectors. By the same token, we should not be surprised that other service industries (such as transportation and trade) that experienced large employment losses due to technological change are missing from this list because the unions had a much weaker bargaining position in these industries.

There is no conclusive evidence that the legislative provisions which exist in some provinces contributed to the level or pace of adjustment in technological change clauses in collective agreements. While Knight (1986, pp. 420 and 421) is assertive on this question, the Economic Council's study on Innovation and Jobs (ECC 1987, p. 115) reaches the opposite conclusion. Both studies agree that little headway has been made in collective bargaining over technological change beyond advance notice and, to a certain extent, training.

The striking lack of progress in negotiating change through joint union-management technological change committees signals to some "the more limited contribution that collective bargaining will be able to make in adjusting to new technology" (Knight 1986, p. 423). It is also noted that the industrial relations response in Canada to technological change is "very often still treated as a competitive or distributive issue in bargaining rather than as having some degree of integrative potential" (Knight 1986, p. 424). Both studies deplore the distributive compulsion in technological change issues in North American industrial relations and compare them to the more favourable consultative procedures available in such jurisdictions as Japan, West Germany or Sweden (ECC 1987, pp. 124-128).

A roundtable conference of industrial relations practitioners dealing with industrial relations expressed considerably more optimism about future co-operative ventures in partnership areas such as technological change (Benimadhu 1986, p. 29 ff), again suggesting inconclusive evidence with respect to the changed prospects in Canadian industrial relations.

Part-Time Workers

The second most pressing issue of industrial relations in the service industries, which is furthermore closely related to the third issue of pay equity and wage discrimination, is the widespread and growing use of part-time work. As has been shown in chapter 2, part-time work has been growing at a faster rate than full-time work. This is largely facilitated by the growth of the service sector. "72% of the part-time workers are women and part-time jobs pay only 79% of full-time jobs, based on an averaging of hourly wage rates across all part-time and full-time jobs" (Labour Canada 1983, p. 21).

In the past, differential pay, fringe benefits, and stability of part-time jobs, together with the potential substitution of part-time for full-time labour and their varying occurrence across industries have met with a rather mixed industrial relations response. While unions have traditionally been opposed to any form of part-time work for reasons of low membership support and perceived threat of substitution, changes have taken place which culminated in the Canadian Labour Congress declaration in 1976 that it would support measures to ensure the equality of part-time and full-time workers.

Generally speaking, union attitudes towards part-time work appear to be strictly a function of the generic composition of their members. Where female workers comprise a large proportion of the membership, as in the case with nurses, teachers, and some specific locals of the RWDS (Retail, Wholesale and Department Store Unions), they have acknowledged the phenomenon and fought with some success to improve working conditions. However, a considerable amount of union ambivalence has been reported among such groups as postal workers, communication workers, and university lecturers and their union representatives. At the other extreme, transit unions still appear to be opposed to the introduction of part-time drivers (Labour Canada 1983, pp. 98-99).

Finally, in opposition to management's insistence on introducing part-time labour on grounds of increasing the efficiency of working time, unions face the added dilemma of having to decide between well remunerated, desirable overtime pay and regular or even marginally paid normal time for different groups of workers which would involve political trade-offs with regard to union membership.[2] Union membership appears to have increased both wages and prorated benefits among part-time workers (Labour Canada 1983, p. 74).

The pay equity issue is closely related to the complex of questions dealing with part-time labour through gender-related forms of employment and wage discrimination. Female/male wage and employment discrimination has a long history both in industrial relations practices and labour market research. The secular rise of female part-time employment, notably in service sector industries, has brought the issue into the forefront of current legislative endeavours and labour policy debates.

This is not the place for a lengthy literature review on either gender-related earning and employment differentials or legal approaches towards equity pay (see Agarwal 1982, ECC 1985, or Jain 1982). What might be important prior to consulting our own evidence on male/female wage differentials in the service sector is to point out the fact that there is a clear link between occupational segregation and the existence of lower earnings for women. This, in turn, has implications not only for the calculation of the proper earnings differential but more so for the correct interpretation of market behaviour and discrimination. Policy implications would clearly be very different if the overcrowding of women into low-paying female jobs were the result of pre-market educational streaming than if it were to arise from differential hiring, training or promotion policies between men and women. Thus, problems can arise both from cultural norms regarding gender roles in the home and in the market as well as from imperfections in the labour market.

Presently, neither union demands nor existing Canadian equal-pay-for-work-of-equal-value legislation have recognized the complexity of the linkage between occupational segregation and wage differentials by sex but have instead tried to assess and equalize pay among men and women based on similar input characteristics (such as skill, education, and effort). Earlier studies have shown differentials to vary from 7 to 45 percent, depending on methodology and sample coverage (Agarwal 1982, pp. 784-785).

The issue of discrimination also appears to be a persistent one (Eberts 1979) which suggests that signs of change have to be interpreted from a longer run and dynamic perspective involving more than mere interpretation of equal pay legislation and its enforcement. Instead, changing access in typically male dominated sectors, occupations, and jobs has to be analysed along with reported wage differentials.

Wages and Income Distribution

Before considering the issue of wage determination and wage developments in service sector industries, it is useful to compare the typical elements and composition of labour costs in a number of service sectors with those prevailing in manufacturing or in the economy as a whole. As can be seen from table 38, service industries span a wide range, including some of the lowest paid sectors (trade and personal, business and community services) but also sectors with the highest average employee compensation (public administration and transportation). Compensation differences are often the result of more generous benefit packages as is reflected, for example, in the lower percentage of basic or straight pay for transportation (70.5 percent) and public administration (73.4 percent) in comparison with education, health, and welfare where basic pay represents 81.6 percent of total compensation.

Most of the information provided by Statistics Canada in table 39 is self-evident and not too surprising. For example, the public sector is the most generous and trade and services the least generous industries with respect to paid absence. Cost of living allowances only play a role in manufacturing

Table 38
Elements and Composition of Total Employee Compensation
Percentage by Industry

Elements of Employee Compensation	Manufacturing	Transportation	Trade	Finance	Education, Health and Welfare	Commercial Services	Public Administration	All Industries
Basic or Straight-Time Pay	71.9	70.5	77.2	73.0	81.6	79.6	73.4	74.6
Commissions and Production Bonuses	1.5	0.5	4.5	7.8	0.7	1.5	—	1.6
Overtime and Holiday Work	4.6	4.5	1.4	1.4	0.1	2.3	2.3	3.2
Shift Premium Pay	0.5	0.5	0.1	—	0.1	—	0.2	0.3
Other Pay for Time Worked	0.2	0.6	—	0.1	0.3	0.1	1.0	0.3
Expenditure for Time Worked	78.7	76.6	83.2	82.3	82.7	83.5	76.9	80.0
Vacation Pay	5.0	5.0	4.5	4.4	4.3	4.4	5.1	4.8
Paid Holidays	3.5	3.3	3.3	3.2	4.2	3.4	3.8	3.6
Sick Leave	0.5	1.3	0.7	1.3	1.6	0.7	2.1	1.0
Other Paid Absence	0.1	0.2	0.1	0.2	0.2	0.1	0.4	0.2
Expenditures for Paid Absence	9.1	9.8	8.6	9.1	10.3	8.6	11.4	9.6
Floating COLA	0.9	0.5	0.1	—	0.1	—	—	0.4
Christmas, Year End Bonus	0.5	0.1	0.7	0.3	—	0.5	—	0.3
Severance Pay	0.1	0.2	0.1	0.2	0.3	0.2	0.4	0.2
Taxable Benefits	1.1	1.0	0.7	0.7	0.5	0.8	0.7	0.9
Other Payments	0.1	0.1	0.1	—	0.2	0.1	0.3	0.2
Expenditures for Miscellaneous Payment	2.7	2.0	1.7	1.2	1.1	1.6	1.4	1.9
Gross Payroll	90.5	88.4	93.5	92.6	94.2	93.7	89.7	91.4
Workers' Compensation	1.7	1.1	0.8	0.1	0.3	0.6	0.4	1.1
Pension Plans CPP, QPP	1.0	0.9	1.1	1.1	1.0	1.2	1.0	1.0
Other	3.1	6.4	1.7	3.2	2.2	1.8	6.2	3.4
Life and Health Insurance	2.2	1.7	1.3	1.5	1.0	1.2	1.4	1.6
Unemployment Insurance	1.3	1.1	1.5	1.4	1.3	1.5	1.3	1.3
Other Benefit Plans	0.2	0.4	0.1	0.1	—	—	—	0.2
Expenditures for Welfare and Benefit Plans	9.5	11.6	6.5	7.4	5.8	6.3	10.3	8.6
Total Average Employee Compensation in 1978	100% ($16,781)	100% ($19,674)	100% ($13,549)	100% ($15,010)	100% ($16,144)	100% ($12,086)	100% ($18,105)	100% ($16,481)

Source: Calculated from Statistics Canada, *Employee Compensation in Canada, All Industries*, 1980, catalogue 72-618, pp. 10–11.

Table 39

Male and Female Rates of Unemployment by Service Sector Industry and Female Unemployment Differentials, 1971 and 1981

| | 1971 | | | | 1981 | | | |
	Male	Female	Female/Male Difference	Total	Male	Female	Female/Male Difference	Total
Industry	(1)	(2)	(2–1)		(1)	(2)	(2–1)	
Manufacturing Industries	5.90	9.00	3.10	6.70	5.20	9.30	4.10	6.30
Transport, Communications and Other Utilities	4.72	5.69	0.97	4.89	4.35	4.89	0.54	4.48
Transportation	5.33	5.92	0.59	5.38	5.13	5.69	0.56	5.22
Storage	5.59	10.64	5.05	6.29	5.10	7.40	2.30	5.52
Communications	3.26	5.61	2.35	4.16	2.76	4.35	1.59	3.42
Electric Power, Gas and Water Utilities	3.59	4.40	0.81	3.69	3.15	3.73	0.58	3.25
Trade	5.13	7.42	2.29	5.97	4.68	6.80	2.12	5.60
Wholesale Trade	4.87	7.89	3.02	5.56	4.28	6.92	2.64	5.03
Retail Trade	5.26	7.33	2.07	6.13	4.91	6.77	1.86	5.83
Finance, Insurance and Real Estate	2.84	5.10	2.26	4.00	2.64	4.02	1.38	3.49
Finance Industries	2.69	4.98	2.29	4.02	2.25	3.88	1.63	3.39
Financial Carriers	2.23	5.22	2.99	3.72	2.22	3.75	1.53	3.13
Insurance Agencies and Real Estate Industry	3.39	5.29	1.90	4.15	3.17	4.53	1.36	3.82
Community, Business and Personal Service	5.26	5.06	-0.20	5.14	5.49	6.63	1.14	6.18
Education and Related Services	2.82	2.51	-0.31	2.65	2.99	4.55	1.56	3.90
Health and Welfare Services	2.81	3.08	0.27	3.01	3.59	4.15	0.56	4.03
Religious Organizations	1.38	2.33	0.95	1.80	2.44	2.61	0.17	2.53
Amusement and Recreation Services	11.16	12.32	1.16	11.55	11.22	12.88	1.66	11.95
Services to Business Management	4.98	7.32	2.34	5.81	4.34	6.58	2.24	5.30
Personal Services	5.10	6.97	1.87	6.39	5.03	7.63	2.60	6.94
Accommodation and Food Services	9.65	10.01	0.36	9.86	8.73	11.52	2.79	10.43
Miscellaneous Services	7.45	7.40	0.05	7.43	7.86	8.80	0.94	8.27
Public Administration and Defence	3.50	3.95	0.45	3.62	4.13	6.42	2.29	4.97
Federal Administration	3.24	3.99	0.75	3.43	3.56	5.42	1.86	4.26
Provincial Administration	3.90	2.79	-1.11	3.53	4.06	6.74	2.68	5.26
Local Administration	3.60	6.21	2.61	4.04	4.95	8.14	3.19	5.81
Other Government Offices	10.92	7.18	-3.74	9.46	10.49	6.37	-4.12	8.07

Source: Statistics Canada, Census, 1971 and 1981.

and transportation, and overtime pay is surprisingly low in the trade sector in view of the seasonal character of most retail and wholesale businesses. The latter likely reflects the extensive use of part-time workers in these industries.

Among the most important factors which have affected real wages in the service sector are changes in technology. The introduction of new information technologies in the service sector has led to a transformation of work organization and skills. This must have had consequences for differential productivity and wage growth among and within service sectors. Unfortunately, data unavailability and productivity measurement problems preclude a closer examination of the nexus between technological change, productivity, and real wage.

Instead, we may test a different though related hypothesis with respect to the wage impact of technological change—the much debated phenomenon of "the declining middle" (Kuttner 1983). Technical changes, notably those in the service industries, have been said to lead to a polarization of skills and earnings and to greater specialization of service expertise both within and across industries. While an exhaustive test of changes in the distribution of Canadian income ultimately must rest on individual wage or income data, partial tests can be performed on disaggregated industry data. Specifically, we can track the changing variance of average industry earnings across manufacturing and service sector industries over a specified period of time and observe the overall impact on the distribution of earnings. This was done for all service sector industries for which data were reported in Employment, Earnings and Hours, Statistics Canada Cat. No. 72-002. Average industry earnings data were subsequently matched with unpublished Statistics Canada employment data for the same SIC industry codes.

The results displayed in figures 1 to 3 are surprising. The Gini index for the service sector as a whole fell over the period 1975 to 1985, as seen in figure 2, yielding a less skewed income distribution (in terms of intra-sectoral variance in earnings) as is also shown in the Lorenz curves for 1975 and 1985 (figure 1). When manufacturing is included, the Gini index rises (see figure 3). Comparing the distribution of industry earnings for manufacturing and the service sector in 1975 and 1985 we obtain:

Comparison of Gini Indices:

Manufacturing	1975 :	.084
	1985 :	.111
Services	1975 :	.28
	1985 :	.202

Figure 1
Lorenz Curve for the Service Sector, 1975 and 1985

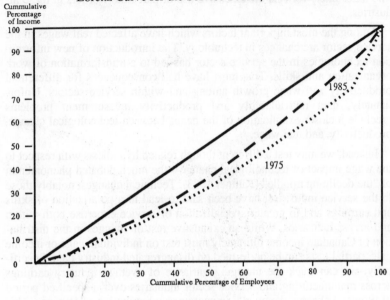

Figure 2
Gini Index for the Service Sector Only, 1975 to 1985

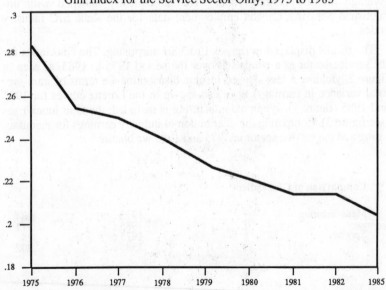

Figure 3
Gini Index Including Manufacturing and Service Sectors, 1975 to 1985

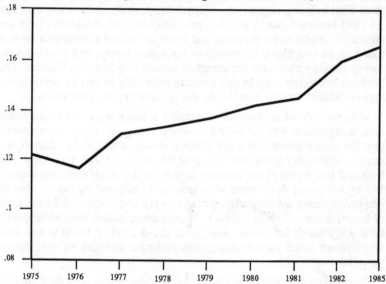

Thus, while there has always been a greater inter-industry variance of earnings in the service sector, it has declined appreciably over the period 1975 to 1985 while the opposite has been true for manufacturing.

The data cannot be used to prove the complete absence of a declining middle as a result of skill polarization within given industries. Average industry earnings may still hide distributional changes in skills and earnings within industries. Nevertheless, the results suggest that the service economy as a whole has not been at the root of large distributional changes in income. Those changes have come from the manufacturing sector.[3] One possible implication of the data is that there may also have been greater inter-industrial mobility of labour in the service sector in contrast to manufacturing. Given the varied determinants of wages and their possible changes over time, this must be interpreted as a speculative suggestion rather than conclusive evidence.

In the analysis of service sector wages, two sets of data were utilized. The first set was average weekly earnings by industry group for Canada from the time series on employment, earnings and hours covering the period 1974 to 1982 (Statistics Canada 72-002). These figures could be matched with detailed unpublished employment figures for the same industry groupings which were provided by Statistics Canada. Industry employment was further broken down by age and sex. The second data set came from unpublished Statistics Canada business microdata, containing three-digit industry figures on employment, payroll, and average earnings for 1983 broken down by age, sex and company size. As distinct from the published employment, earnings, and hours series, the second data set was based on an integration of individual tax return figures and establishment survey results which were subsequently matched by Statistics Canada. The business microdata used in this analysis refer only to service sector earnings in Ontario, thereby eliminating any possible regional variations.

With the help of the first set of industry average wage and employment data, a regression was developed in which changing employment characteristics were regressed on wage levels and wage changes. In addition, our sample of industry groupings was split into service sector industries with high and low levels of unionization to test for the union effect on wages.[4] We hypothesized that wages were negatively affected by the number of employed young workers and females and positively affected by the level of unionization in a given industry. Regression equations were utilized with both wage levels and wage changes as the dependent variable and with employment ratios for various groups and ratio changes as independent variables.

Before commenting on the results, a few observations regarding the data and methodology are in order. As is shown by a mushrooming literature on the estimation of earnings functions, extreme care has to be taken in obtaining unbiased estimates of earnings differentials associated with specific individual worker, firm, or market characteristics. The situation is further complicated by the presence of two wage earners, maximizing family (as opposed to individual) income, and by the presence of unobservable individual and organizational traits affecting productivity and earnings (Nakamura and Nakamura 1985). But even if it were possible to statistically match individual and family earnings data with information on productivity characteristics among workers and employers and use them in a simultaneous equation model, problems of causality determination and interpretation remain. It would still be necessary to know the underlying and varying objectives of firms regarding employment and utilization of human capital and its expected term structure. Take, for example, the employment of youths 15-24 years of age. Firms may employ a disproportionate number of youths, either because they need a very mobile and flexible work force due to strong seasonal fluctuations in demand, because they only offer unskilled work commanding teenage wages, or because firms want to develop a skilled labour force by providing training while paying lower wages.

Before it is possible to specify a particular functional form for the earnings equation and prescribe causality between demographic characteristics, productivity, employment, and earnings, more information is needed regarding the varying objectives and length of planning horizons of human resource management. As with other parts of this study, no attempts were made to obtain new results or develop new methodologies. The goal was to reconfirm conclusions and results obtained elsewhere using a simplified reduced form regression equation. The two best regression results in terms of both theoretical expectations and statistical fit are reported below.

1) $\quad$ AVINDWAG $\quad=\quad$ 395.0 - 6.58 RATYG - 3.53 RATOLDFEM

$\qquad\qquad\qquad\qquad$ (28.9) $\quad$ (-16.05) $\qquad$ (-7.13)

$\qquad\qquad$ + .214 RATYGFEM/MALE + 23.8 TIME

$\qquad\qquad$ (6.37) $\qquad\qquad\qquad$ (15.76)

$\qquad\qquad$ ADJUSTED R2 = .895

$\qquad\qquad$ DURBIN WATSON = 1.8

2) $\quad$ AVINDWAG $\quad=\quad$ 383 - 6.39 RATYG - 3.44 RATOLDFEM

$\qquad\qquad\qquad\qquad$ (20.68) (-13.9) $\qquad$ (-6.83)

$\qquad\qquad$ + .22 RATYGFEM/MALE + 23.7 TIME + 8.62 UNION

$\qquad\qquad$ (6.43) $\qquad\qquad\qquad$ (15.74) $\qquad\quad$ (.93)

$\qquad\qquad$ ADJUSTED R2 = .895

$\qquad\qquad$ DURBIN WATSON = 1.72

$\qquad\qquad$ t statistics in parentheses

AVINDWAG	=	Average weekly earnings by industry group for Canada, (April) 1974-1982
RATYG	=	percentage of youth employment (15-24) in given industry groups
RATOLDFEM	=	percentage of female employment (25 and over) in given industry groups
RATYGFEM/ MALE	=	Ratio of young female to young male employment in given industry groupings
TIME	=	Shift parameter for years 1974 = 1, 2, 3 . . . .
UNION	=	Dummy variable for unionization with low union density = 0

As expected, both the presence of young workers and adult female workers depress average wages. For example, a one percentage point change in the ratio of adult female employment lowers the average weekly industry earnings by $3.53, a one percentage point rise in the employment ratio of youth lowers it by $6.53 (equation 1).

A somewhat surprising result was the performance of RATYG-FEM/MALE, the ratio of young females relative to young males in given industry groups. More importantly, this variable contributed over 25 percent of the explained variance and was statistically significant in both regressions. A possible interpretation and one which would be consistent with earlier results on labour and labour substitution (Weiermair 1986) would read as follows: over time there has probably been a reduction in wage discrimination against women which, however, does not apply equally to all age categories. Indeed, older women who have either re-entered the work-force or had less exposure to education and training may be paid substantially below rates which are offered to men in the same age group and industry category. On the other hand, young women who are entering the labour force with similar or higher levels of education are paid above industry averages. We may have a situation where increasing the ratio of young female workers can raise average industry earnings while raising the share of older females would tend to lower it. Since women typically receive higher returns to education but lower returns to years of experience (Boyd and Humphreys 1979, p. 32), and since employers have a tendency to substitute female adult labour for youths in low skill, low paying jobs (Weiermair 1986, p. 482), our results may not be so surprising after all. As can be seen from equation 2, high levels of unionization affect average earnings, but the coefficient is both small and statistically insignificant.

These results have to be interpreted with utmost caution as they are likely to involve a downward bias due to the data and methodology which was used. The choice of sample period (1974 to 1982) and the fact that unionization was entered as a binary variable rather than being expressed as a percentage of union density have likely accounted for these low estimates of union effects. Elsewhere, unionization has been found to add between 16 and 51 percent to average Canadian wages (Diewert 1974, MacDonald 1983). When corrected for omitted variables, union effects still amount to a respectable average of 10.5 percent (Kumar and Stengos 1985, p. 186).

The second data set, although very rich in detail with respect to industry coverage, employee characteristics and establishment data,[5] had one major drawback in that it recorded average annual pay only. The latter was arrived at by blending T4-tax and establishment survey information, which did not allow for an adequate treatment of part-time workers and part-time pay. Although Statistics Canada provided subsequent data which were to represent the full year equivalent (FYE) number of employees on payroll, we were advised at the time not to use the FYE numbers because they were unreliable. Therefore, while our calculations show some interesting results with respect to the variability of annual earnings across service sector industries, age groups, and size of establishment (and any cross-classification thereof), our reported wage differentials will show biases wherever disproportionate numbers of part-time workers are involved. This is particularly true for differences in female and male earnings. Downward biases are also likely to be found among the categories of youth and older employees, which include more than proportionate numbers of part-time workers. Another possibility which could account for the lower annual earnings of workers in small firms and hence for the downward bias are higher rates of employee turnover in smaller establishments (due to higher corporate turnover rates) and associated phenomena of part-year workers.

Table 40

Regression Results for Average (annual) Pay in 48 Service Sector Industries in Ontario in 1983

Variable	Parameter Estimate	t-Value
Intercept	15,631.83	10.95
Sex (Female)	−6,121.34	−7.73*
Age 0–14	−8,173.09	−5.52*
15–24	−5,309.18	−3.58*
25–34	1,161.52	0.78
35–44	5,711.50	3.85*
45–54	7,388.84	4.99*
55–64	5,967.40	4.03*
65+ (Base)	—	
Firm Size		
1–4.9 Employees	−7,409.69	−5.40*
1–19.9 Employees	−4,350.93	−3.17*
20–49.9 Employees	−2,103.05	−1.53
50–99.9 Employees	−1,760.92	−1.28
100–499.9 Employees	−1,079.41	−0.79
500+ (Base)	—	

Note: * Statistically significant at the 1 percent level or better; adjusted R^2 = .804

The results displayed in table 40 are not surprising and behave like most other earnings functions. There is a large differential for sex (but note the presence of part-time work). The pay-off to age or experience is normally behaved as suggested by the peaking of earnings in the 55-64 age category,[6] and there are increasing returns to firm size which again is generally found in earnings functions. Although not all of the employer size-related variables were statistically significant, we note large average pay differences between the smallest and largest companies. Indeed, in many cases pay differentials (holding age and sex constant) between companies employing 1-5 workers and those having 500-plus employees amounted to 200 percent or more. Even if we allow for some bias, noise, or both in the data, as well as labour market imperfections, this still suggests that large productivity differentials must exist between very large and very small companies. This has rather dramatic implications for the industrial organization of service sector industries in terms of economies of scale and the future concentration potential of this sector.

In order to throw additional light on the possible variability of company size-related earnings differences across different industries, average earnings cross-classified by age, and company size in six different three-digit service industries (food stores, pressers and cleaners, security brokers, computer services, hospitals, and universities and colleges) were analysed. The earlier observation of pay differences across company size was similarly present in intra-industry pay comparisons. Depending on the age category, they varied between 200 to 400 percent, irrespective of industry. The only noticeable difference was a delayed peaking of age earnings profiles (around 65+) in industries such as hospitals and universities and colleges and an earlier peaking for computer services and brokerage firms (in the 20-49.9 age category). Again, this is what would be expected in terms of the typical acquisition and depreciation pattern of human capital across these service sector industries.

While we cannot rule out biases due to the distribution of part-time and part-year workers across different sizes of companies, the consistency and size of the pay premium in companies which employ 500 or more people warrants further research in order to shed light on the question of inter-firm labour productivity differences.

Labour Market Frictions—Unemployment and Shortages

Analyses of past technological and structural changes within the service sector were provided in chapter 4. Among the conclusions of that section was an observation of possible qualitative mismatches of supply and demand associated with a dynamically changing mix of skill requirements due to technical changes and a lagged institutional response in the production and provision of skills. The theme of labour market frictions in the service sector will be taken up again in this chapter with an analysis of service sector unemployment and shortages.

Tables 41 to 43 provide an overview of unemployment rates in major service sector groups in comparison to manufacturing, and of unemployment rates in major occupational categories, along with more disaggregated service sector industry unemployment figures broken down by sex for the two census years 1971 and 1981. As can be seen from table 41, Canada's service sector has historically shown lower rates of unemployment and lower cyclical swings in its unemployment rate in comparison with manufacturing, construction, or the primary sector (not shown in the table). This situation is changing as most recent service sector unemployment rates have edged up and are approaching those in other sectors of the economy.

Table 41

Unemployment Rate by Industry, 1975 to 1986

Year	Manufacturing Total	Transportation, Communications, and Utilities	Finance, Insurance, Real Estate	Trade	Public Administration
1975	7.3	5.1	5.4	5.9	4.2
1976	8.0	5.2	6.6	6.3	5.1
1977	8.1	6.9	7.4	7.8	5.6
1978	7.1	5.8	7.7	7.3	6.4
1979	7.1	4.8	7.1	6.2	6.1
1980	7.7	4.9	6.6	6.5	5.7
1981	10.1	5.4	6.8	7.4	5.4
1982	15.5	9.0	9.2	11.4	7.0
1983	11.3	7.3	10.2	9.7	7.8
1984	10.4	7.5	10.1	9.4	8.9
1985	8.9	7.4	9.6	8.8	8.3
1986	8.8	6.6	8.8	8.2	7.7

Source: Historical Labour Force Statistics, Statistics Canada, catalogue 71-201, p. 22.

In terms of the aforementioned structural changes, service sector unemployment should be affected by both industry and occupational shifts. Occupational shifts toward certain managerial and professional categories, for example, would imply higher employment growth for these categories and consequently a lower rate of unemployment in these occupations. However, the hypothesized negative trade-off between growth in occupational employment and the occupational unemployment rate is likely to vary with general business conditions. The higher the general rate of un-

employment the larger will be the rate of unemployment in declining occupations (Gershuny and Miles 1983, p. 67).

Industry employment growth, however, is likely to be differently related
to the rate of unemployment in the same sector. Indeed, if structural changes are pronounced and lead to a major intra- and inter-industry re-alloca-
tion of labour, it is possible that periods of large employment expansion
will also be associated with the simultaneous existence of unemployment in
the same expanding sectors. Employment growth in varying service sector
occupations and industries for ten-, four-, and one-year periods between
1971 and 1981 were correlated with the occupational and/or industrial unemployment rate in 1981. No correlation or only small positive correlations
resulted from relating services sector employment growth to the industry
unemployment rate in 1981. (The correlation coefficient was 0.022 for correlations with industry employment changes covering the period 1971 to
1981 and 0.12 with a one-year employment change figure for the period
1980 to 1981.) Both the presence of a positive correlation coefficient and
its decline with longer reference periods of employment change point to
structural elements of unemployment. They are associated with technical
changes in the service sector. The evidence fits equally well with earlier
observations of lagging adjustments in the retraining and re-education of
workers and the slow adjustment of education and training systems to new
labour market demands.

Turning to occupational unemployment, appreciable differences both
over time, across occupations, and between sexes can be found (see tables
42 and 43). To test the hypothesis of an inverse relationship between the
rate of unemployment and previous long-term employment growth within
occupational categories, the occupational unemployment rate in 1981 and
the occupational employment growth rate for the period 1971 to 1981 are
recorded for all workers and both sexes in table 43.

While it is possible to construct an inverse relationship between occupational employment growth and the occupational unemployment rate for all
workers,' this relationship does not hold when correlating sex-specific rates
of employment growth and occupational unemployment. Female rates are
generally higher in those industries or occupations where women have
achieved considerable employment growth. Both tables 42 and 43 show the
worsening of female unemployment, most notably in the public sector, in a
number of community, business, and personal service industries and in
such occupational groupings as natural sciences, sales, and clerical. This
trend seems to have continued in the eighties, as can be seen from the 1986
figures provided in table 41. "Just as female employment has tended to
grow faster in those particular occupations where female labour productivity has experienced above-average changes in percentage terms"
(Postner and Wesa 1987, p. 91), female unemployment has also grown

Table 42
Unemployment Rate by Occupation

	1978		1981		1986	
	Male	Female	Male	Female	Male	Female
Managerial and Administrative	2.8	2.5	1.7	3.1	3.7	5.5
Natural Sciences	4.4	4.0	2.5	—	6.4	9.2
Social Sciences	4.8	—	—	4.6	—	5.8
Religion	—	—	—	—	—	—
Teaching	3.1	—	—	3.4	2.9	3.9
Medicine and Health	4.1	—	—	2.2	—	4.2
Artistic and Recreational	7.4	7.4	8.7	7.8	11.0	11.0
Clerical	7.5	6.8	5.4	6.0	6.9	8.1
Sales	6.6	4.6	3.9	6.3	6.3	9.6
Services	11.8	10.9	8.0	11.1	12.5	13.0
Agriculture	7.5	6.9	5.6	6.3	7.9	8.7
Fishing, Hunting, et cetera	—	—	11.9	—	14.4	—
Forestry and Logging	33.4	33.3	39.5	—	47.0	—
Mining and Quarrying	13.4	13.3	10.9	—	20.6	—
Processing	10.1	7.5	8.8	18.3	9.7	22.3
Machining	10.8	10.2	6.7	—	11.7	—
Product Fabricating	10.2	7.9	5.8	12.3	8.9	12.7
Construction Trades	23.0	23.0	15.4	—	20.3	—
Transport Equipment Operating	9.4	9.6	10.3	—	13.0	—
Material Handling	14.0	12.3	11.9	11.0	15.4	13.7
Other Crafts and Equipment Operating	5.5	4.7	—	12.8	6.0	12.6

Source: Statistics Canada, The Labour Force, April, various issues, catalogue 71-001.

Table 43
Percentage Growth Rate in Occupational Employment, 1971 to 1981

	Growth Rate in Occupational Employment, 1971–81			Unemployment Rate in 1981 (April)		
Occupational Groups	Total	Male	Female	Total	Male	Female
Managerial and Administrative	133	122	189	2.1	1.7	3.1
Natural Sciences	29	18.9	90.7	2.7	2.5	—
Teaching Occupations	51.1	54.3	48.4	2.2	—	3.4
Artistic and Recreational	68.8	49.6	108.4	8.4	8.7	7.8
Clerical	56.2	12.4	75.1	5.9	5.4	6.0
Sales	44.9	23.3	74.3	4.8	3.9	6.3
Material Handling and Packaging	8.6	6.7	14.6	11.7	11.9	11.0

Source: Sex specific occupational employment growth from Postner and Wesa, p. 61ff, and Unemployment Rates from Statistics Canada, catalogue 71-001.

faster in those occupations where, in comparison to males, females recorded higher rates of employment growth.

A number of competing explanations can be offered: (a) women are the victims of technological change due to pure prejudice and discrimination; (b) women suffer higher rates of technological unemployment due to human capital considerations (such as lower relative expected payoffs to the firm from experience and training); (c) there may be a surplus of female workers in certain occupations due to rigid wages or other rigidities in institutional labour market arrangements (such as enforcement of pay equity in case of unequal work value); and (d) women previously dropped out of the labour force when unemployed, now they stay in and get counted.

With the existence of less than perfect product or service markets, pure discrimination cannot be ruled out. Some unemployment is likely to be associated with sex-related labour supply differences such as educational attainment, previous work experience, and mobility traits. *A priori* one would expect less institutional and wage rigidity to exist among female workers because of their lower levels of unionization and the higher proportion of part-time workers among women. From existing data it is not possible to know how much of the rising unemployment differentials have come from a discriminatory crowding out of female workers and how much may have been the result of differential labour quality. This would be a fruitful area for future research.

Turning to the question of occupational shortages, reliance has to be placed on periodic employer surveys and task forces on training which typically yield softer and more qualitative evidence. Only a few industrial and occupational categories, such as information and communication services, computer programmers and analysts, engineers, and health care personnel, appeared on the list of service sector industries or occupations with shortages in the late 1970s and early 1980s (ECC 1982, p. 37 ff). This situation appears to have changed during the latter part of the 1880s, according to both the Ontario Task Force on Employment and New Technology (1985) and the Background Industry Information for the Ontario Services Sector Study (1986). Both reports forecast shortages during the latter part of the eighties due to a new generation of technologies being applied in a number of service sector industries and educational institutions being unable, and at times unwilling, to follow industry trends. At the same time, both studies indicate redundancies in clerical and secretarial occupations. At least in Ontario, expected shortages are widely distributed over specific service sector industries (table 44).

The same employer surveys showed that firms attempted to solve shortage problems through such firm-internal measures as more vigorous efforts in the recruitment of technical and engineering skills, upgrading administrative skills, and retraining. The firms' response appears rational.

Table 44

Expected Occupational Shortages in Ontario

Industry	Managerial, Administration and Related	Computer Programmers and Analysts	Engineers, Technicians	Sales Supervisors	Sales and Sales	Bookkeepers, Accounting and EDP Operators	Financial Management
Telecommunications	X	X	X				
Computer Services	X	X		X			
Management Consulting	X	X		X			
Banks	X					X	X
Trust and Loan Companies	X		X		X		
Retail Food Stores	X			X	X		
General Merchandise Stores	X		X	X	X		
Life Insurance	X		X				
General Insurance	X						X
Insurance Agents and Brokers		X			X		

Source: *The Ontario Task Force on Employment and New Technology*, 1985; *Employment and New Technology in Ontario's Service Sector*, 1986, *Ontario Study of the Service Sector, Industry Profile.* and Ministry of Treasury and Economics.

The risks and costs of human resource development and the increased firm specificity of administrative skills are lower than those associated with engineers and technologists or technicians, whose human capital formation is both more general and more costly, and thus represent a higher human capital risk for employers. Again, this highlights the previously mentioned problem of the adjustments needed in Canadian systems of education and training.

Summary

Until very recently, industrial relations development in the service sector has been characterized by a steady increase in union density. Pay equity, part-time work and job security, particularly as it relates to the introduction of new technologies, have been the dominant issues in collective bargaining. So far, discussion on the economic rationale, economic effects, and ideal legal provisions underlying part-time work and pay equity have engaged many task forces, commissions of inquiry and research reports without yielding a consensus among researchers or interest groups. The design of effective labour market laws and policies which could address such problems as discrimination or female dominated part-time work has been hampered in part by the complexity of the issues at hand, the multi-varied nature of their determination, and their variability across different service sector industries.

We expect some of these problems to sort themselves out without intervention as there appears to be a general trend towards increased flexibility of working time and gender-related wage and employment differences appear headed towards a long-run decline. Evidence of the industrial relations response to technological change has been equally inconclusive with the exception of its recognized inferiority relative to some foreign experience.

Some interesting and rather positive results have been obtained from tests of the "declining middle" hypothesis. Tests for the past decade showed a fall in the Gini index (as a measure of inequality) of the service sector relative to manufacturing. This suggests that whatever polarization of earnings may have occurred in the Canadian economy over the recent past, it has not originated in the service sector. On the contrary, the higher mobility and flexibility of labour markets in the service industries have contributed to lower earning differentials in the long run. Subsequent and limited analyses of wage behaviour have provided the usual and expected results in terms of sex and age-related wage differentials as well as well-behaved age-earnings profiles. More surprising has been the observation of small wage effects associated with unionization and the large earning differentials associated with the size of employing establishment.

Labour market frictions in the form of unemployment and shortages have worsened over the past 15 years. This has been true for unemployment in the service sector in general but even more so for female service sector unemployment. Most employer surveys indicated the existence of skill shortages which may imply structural mismatches due to rapid technological change and lagging adjustments in the general system of education and training.

NOTES

1.   Informal management/labour agreements on technological change are likely to exist in the non-unionized service sector, particularly the high technology segment. This finding is corroborated by evidence from a separate count on technological change clauses in agreements by Facts on the Current Industrial Relations Scene (Industrial Relations Centre 1987).

2.   A good discussion of the related issues of overtime, part-time work, and flexibility in working time can be found in Ontario Task Force on Hours of Work and Overtime (1987).

3.   Possible reasons for the declining middle in the service sector would be increased feminization of work, changing age distribution towards younger workers, or technical change. Evidence on the absence of a declining middle has also been found in the Economic Council of Canada's study on Innovation and Jobs, Ibid. pp. 58-68.

4.   The following industry groupings were classified as having a low level of unionization: wholesale and retail trade, finance, insurance and real estate, amusement and recreation, services to business management, personal services, and accommodation and food services. All other service industries were classified as having a high level of unionization.

5.   The data set covered male and female average annual pay classified by seven different age and six different employer size categories for industries at the three-digit SIC code of industrial classification.

6.   There are, however, differences in the behaviour of age/earnings profiles across different service sector industries.

7.   The inverse relationship is strengthened if high unemployment occupations in primary, processing, and construction fields with small or negative employment changes are added to the list.

Chapter 6

LABOUR ADJUSTMENT IN SERVICE SECTOR ORGANIZATIONS: TWO CASE STUDIES

The two case histories reproduced below do not cover the entire spectrum of labour issues and problems in the service sector; nevertheless, they are good examples to study the common trends discussed in chapters 1 through 5.

The choice of study sites was largely determined by resource constraints and the willingness of organizations to co-operate. Ideally, the two case studies should have come from firms at either extreme of the technology level continuum, yielding a typical "high-tech" and a typical "low-tech" service sector organization. As it turned out, both companies operate in the medium to high technology range. Both companies are relatively young and have grown rapidly. This is typical of many services organizations that have benefited from this sector's rapid growth in the post-war period. Finally, both firms experienced technical changes typical of the transformation of the service sector in the past 15 years.

Company A

Company A is an organization in the entertainment and communications industry which produces and sells broadcasting, cable TV, and other communication services. It developed over a relatively short period from a regional cable TV company into the world's largest cable TV company. The company's spectacular growth was in part a function of a dynamic environment which provided for rapid technological changes in ever shortened product and service cycles. Among those major changes were the territorial and capacity extension of cable TV, the introduction of pay TV, and new forms of data transmission. A further driving force behind production and distribution changes has been the constant upgrading and introduction of increasingly sophisticated technologies, such as stereo and digital TV.

What are the major implications of this growth pattern for the overall organization design, work organization, and human resource development? Sales growth, in terms of new client groups and territorial expansion, led to an increase in the organization's division of labour and, consequently, a greater degree of specialization and departmentalization. At the same time, computerization enabled better integration, centralization, and control of corporate activities. The introduction and better use of telecommunications equipment further reduced the firm's need to operate separate branch offices. This enabled the company to centralize consumer services in Toronto. Computerization, which eventually led to a fully integrated information system, reduced the relative number of clerical personnel (particularly statistical clerks and telephone operators) and increased the need for workers with multiple skills (for example, through the merging of marketing and technical functions).

In response to the organization's product cycle, the job and occupational structure changed from a strong marketing orientation to a stronger production orientation as the firm recently committed major resources for rebuilding its technology. This will be followed by another expansion of the marketing function. Among the implications of this growth pattern was a secular increase in the average educational attainment of workers which helped accommodate the requirement for multiple skills to accommodate the overall work-force to the changed pattern of growth and the internal demands of the organization.

The company relied on a careful recruitment and screening strategy, followed by extensive promotion from within, to secure its desired level and mix of human resources. In the case of clerical and semi-managerial skills, this was achieved by usually hiring female part-time workers into a pool from which workers were promoted into full-time entry level clerical positions. This allowed the firm to perform some screening for productivity potential and promotability at low cost. Top professional and managerial functions (such as engineers and executive management) were hired from outside the organization. Finally, intermediate technical skills, such as those of technicians and technologists, were typically recruited from community colleges.

It was with this category of technical workers that company officials expressed some concerns of inadequate supply. Despite better pay in comparison with administrative clerks (and for the same level of schooling), it was difficult to obtain a sufficient number of job applicants. The company believed that the problem was due to low levels of enrolment in technologist and technician programmes, the industry's specificity of skills, and the colleges' lack of curriculum response to recent changes in the skill profile for communications technologists. The proportion of female to male workers was 70 to 30 in clerical positions and 30 to 70 in programming jobs. The presence of female workers in maintenance, repair, and other technical jobs had been practically zero as community colleges apparently could not attract sufficient numbers of female students to male-dominated technologist programmes.

The company's training programmes were geared to upgrading technical skills in areas of technological change. This was accomplished with the help of manufacturing firms (e.g., the suppliers of CAD/CAM systems). In addition, the company provided its workers with financial assistance in further off-the-job training and educational programmes. Management training was provided through an in-house training function.

The company reported few industrial relations problems, and these were only with the unionized portion of its work-force, technical support workers (such as maintenance and repair). The only serious manpower issue, according to the representative of the firm's human resource division, was the serious shortage of technicians and technologists.

The structural evolution of the human organization and the typical pattern of labour adjustment in this organization can probably be best recreated in terms of some of the labour adjustment issues raised earlier in this study.

Technological Change

As is probably typical for many service sector organizations in the medium to high technology field, this firm has been in the centre of technical changes both as a creator of technological change on the product side and as a receiver of technological change in its own operation on the input side. The development of new products, such as pay TV, data transmission, stereo TV, and other differentiated home products, has become an ongoing concern with a product cycle of approximately five years. The most recent product changes to move into the field of data transmission and rebuild facilities will require the commitment of well over $25 million. Organizationally, this has meant a re-orientation towards more engineering, with the attendant questions of where and how to acquire skills and how to best integrate engineering with other key organizational functions, notably marketing.

With respect to adjustments in the composition of skills, the company's general human resources strategy has been one of hiring additionally required engineers, technicians, and technologists as required. They have also supplemented this method of skill acquisition with employer-sponsored training programmes (four full-time, in-house trainers) in order to provide for industry- and organization-specific skills and to better integrate technical and administrative skills. The company has been somewhat reluctant to overextend its training function since most of the skills in question are only industry-specific and hence only transferable to other organizations in the industry.

Community colleges have, on the other hand, not been able to keep up with rapid technological changes in general and in industry-specific developments in particular. A good case in point and one raised in interviews with the company has been that of skills associated with the development of CAD/CAM systems in the telecommunications industry. The integration and transfer of technical and administrative (largely marketing) skills was achieved through such organizational developments as further training, cross-learning, and a strengthening of alternate forms of team production. The ultimate objective was to create multiple skills while simultaneously raising technical and marketing competence throughout the work-force. On the input side, computerization has been the major driving force for changes in the skill composition and work organization. It had the effect of substituting capital and upgraded or multiple skills (more educated or better trained clerical staff) for lower level skills (for example, statistical clerks) and of changing the responsibility and skill level of others (for example, clerical personnel in customer services).

Part-Time Female Employment

Given a relatively abundant supply of female workers, the high costs of screening and hiring due to limited screening capabilities of Canadian educational institutions, and the high costs and risks of human capital functions (on the job learning, training, and further training), the firm established an organization internal labour market. Female workers enter the system as (largely involuntary) part-time workers at relatively low wages. When they have successfully passed initial screening, they are promoted to better paid full-time jobs. Put differently, female workers pay for their own screening and hiring cost, which is somewhat similar to traditional apprenticeship training where workers pay for their own training through lower wages during indenture. Both the constraints of minimum market wages and an insufficient and lagged response in the system of education have led to the establishment of a new entry point in the form of part-time employment.

Company B

Company B is a publicly traded newspaper company which, since its formation 15 years ago, has experienced a dramatic growth from zero to $3 million in revenues and from 60 employees to 1,500 at present. As with Company A, the firm's growth necessitated a fair amount of departmentalization. Company B decided to maintain a far larger amount of decentralized decision making and handled its major products under unified product management with the help of self-contained profit centres. Only finance and corporate planning were centralized in the firm's head office.

This firm also reported a drive toward having most of its activities computerized. The only manpower changes resulting from this growth and technical change process were: (a) a general upgrading of skills in terms of the average educational attainment and general computer literacy of new-hires compared to employees who have been with the company from its inception; (b) rearrangement of jobs between editors, journalists, and compositors, with the effect of reducing the relative importance of typing and composition skills as reporters became responsible for a greater portion of the final product. With the future introduction of fully computerized graphics, the role of compositors is expected to further decline; and (c) a modest amount of contracting out with respect to newspaper distribution which, in contrast with other major newspapers, is handled by independent contractors.

In order to deal with regular workload peaks, the company employs a small number of regular part-time office workers who voluntarily accept a reduced workload. For extraordinary seasonal peaks or special activities (such as the sorting and mailing of flyers), the company avails itself of the services of specialized employment agencies.

Little training is provided, promotion occurs from within the company, and recruitment is done through a number of entry points spaced at various levels in the hierarchy of positions. Major emphasis is placed on maintaining an environment of high achievement, motivation, and "intrapreneurial" corporate culture. To a large measure, this is achieved through decentralized decision making, profit sharing, and the provision of generous company benefits. When asked about experienced and expected manpower imbalances, company officials reported that these were not issues. Indeed, the company suggested that it foresaw few major changes of its non-unionized labour force beyond the manpower adjustments mentioned above. Most skill requirement changes were marginal and developed over longer periods of time (for example, the increased use of financial analysis and skills) and thus could be acquired through a combination of on-the-job learning and job reassignments.

Although this firm has been involved in structural changes to a much lesser degree than Company A and thus offers less case material on quality changes in its work organization and skill profiles, it may nevertheless be instructive to highlight some of its handling of the labour adjustment issues touched upon in the study.

Technological Change and Employment Growth

Being in the information processing field, Company B has been heavily in-volved in the process of computerization both on its production side (intro-duction of mechanized composition and computer graphics) and in its administrative functions (movement toward a centralized computer system with on-line capabilities for key functions and separate profit centres).

Structural change (re-organization) and variability in the pattern of employment growth were smaller on two accounts. As there are very few industry specific skills, a trend toward professionalization in this company simply means higher levels of education for its work-force. With the secular rise of educational attainment among Canadian workers, this was relatively easy to obtain. Being a very young company and having seen most of its growth occur within the past eight years meant that few internal changes were needed. The company was able to gradually and incremental-ly change the composition of its work-force through additional hires in tan-dem with its growth in sales. While there has been some promotion from within the organization, training was minimal. Many of the professional and managerial functions were typically filled through outside hiring.

Female and Part-Time Employment

Company B's recruitment and employment pattern for its female workers was very different from that observed in Company A. Given the far greater importance of seasonal, weekly, and daily peak workloads, there has been a greater demand for permanent part-time workers. The use of permanent part-time, largely female, workers helped smooth out short-run peak loads. Thus, production patterns and the smoothing of work times were, in this case, far more important considerations for the increase in part-time employment than labour cost or screening considerations (Company A). Only where part-time work was very irregular and transaction costs of employment very high, did the company decide to contract out to employ-ment agencies (for example, work associated with the production and mail-ing of advertisement flyers).

Summary

Two cases, particularly when chosen in terms of availability rather than by design, are a poor testing ground for hypotheses. Nevertheless, they help to demonstrate the point which was made earlier with respect to the testability and usefulness of labour market time series data. Secular changes in the qualitative composition of the work-force in the service sector, even when disaggregated by industry, are difficult to interpret without a deeper understanding of the underlying changes in service production. Even similar technological changes, such as computerization, can yield dramatically different work organization and employment effects, as was evident in the two companies studied. Similarly, there may be different reasons for a common phenomenon such as the prevalence of part-time employment.

While it is possible to anticipate and conceptualize possible causes of part-time employment (Weiermair 1987), it is often difficult to know *a priori* when to use which causal factor. Again, the evidence from companies A and B illustrates this point quite well. Without prior case study knowledge, it would have been virtually impossible to infer the exact nature and economic reasons for part-time employment in companies A and B. Having had considerable access to case studies in other equally developed countries helped considerably with the organization and interpretation of Canadian labour market data for the service sector.

SUMMARY AND CONCLUSIONS

Chapter 7 recapitulates the main findings of the study regarding the adjustment of labour in the Canadian service economy, highlights major policy implications, and points out fruitful avenues for future research.

Major Findings

Similar to other industrialized countries, Canada's economy has seen a major restructuring over the past 15 years because of the spectacular growth in its service sector industries. A multiplicity of factors including increased wealth, secular increases in the stock of consumer durables, secularly rising female labour force participation roles, lower transaction costs obtained through contracting out, and deregulation and increased international tradeability in services have all contributed to the recent buoyancy in demand for services and the rising level of employment in this sector. At the same time, this sector both created and was subject to major technological and organizational changes in the form of new information technologies and altered forms of work organization (contractual and part-time work, and co-operation between service organizations). In such a dynamically growing sector, the performance from both intra- and inter-industrial perspectives has been far from uniform. This is also reflected in varied employment growth and the pattern of labour adjustment across different service sector industries. Vast differences have been noted in both the quantitative and compositional changes of employment across such subsectors as producer, personal, and non-commercial services.

Given the magnitude and rapidity of change, labour markets and the education and training system have not been able to adjust fully. It appears that qualitative changes in the supply of labour through alternative forms of skill acquisition (immigration, education, and private and public training) have not been as large or as rapid as one would have expected given the rise of the service economy. In addition to simple inertia, the lagged response has also been caused by short-sighted government policies (such as changes in immigration laws), by a system of educational financing which hampers efficient resource allocation and fosters "grantsmanship," and by adherence to union wage laws which aggravate employer-sponsored forms of training.

On the other hand, employment growth in the service sector has demonstrated a remarkable quantitative flexibility in adjusting to changed economic circumstances. This has been demonstrated by the disproportionate growth of entrepreneurship and small business formation; the arrangement of new types of employment in the form of contracting out, sub-contracting, part-time work and remote employment; and the absorption of the fastest growing labour force groups of women and youth.

In contrast to the rigidities of labour markets in the goods producing sector, labour markets serving the service industries demonstrated much more flexibility and adjustment potential and as such have contributed greatly to Canada's macroeconomic performance in the past decade.[1]

Policy Questions

This study and others have shown that technology (notably information technology) and human capital are the driving supply forces of service sector growth. From a policy perspective, this raises the questions of why innovation in service sector activities has proceeded at different speeds in different industries and how innovation can best be aided. A discussion of policy options and alternatives with respect to the diffusion of technology is beyond the scope of this study and has been dealt with elsewhere in the service sector project. A number of policy questions regarding human capital formation will have to be addressed in the future. A typical sample would include the following issues.

First, has our education system kept pace with the changes in technology and skill requirements typical of a growing and internationally competitive service sector? If the answer is negative, how can we improve the static and dynamic efficiencies of our education system? Policy options may include changes in financing education such as the introduction of a voucher system and greater standardization and control of curriculum developments.

Secondly, how can both private and publicly-sponsored training be organized and financed to respond to the changing demands of the service sector? Again, policy considerations would have to be given to changes in financing training (e.g., lowering minimum wages in favour of an outright educational allowance analogous to traditional apprenticeship programmes), and the desirable level and variability of regulation (Weiermair 1984).

Finally, governments may want to re-examine whether in the past they have received sufficient immigrants to cover both short- and long-run labour market shortages and what, if anything, can be done to increase the match between immigration and the changing skill requirements of the Canadian economy.

Since competition in many services means competition in human capital intensive products, the adjustment of labour has to be viewed largely as a qualitative adjustment. Free trade and globalization of services trade will intensify this process and lay open the relative strength and competitiveness of the education and training system among competing countries. While economists and policy-makers in Canada have recognized the general importance of human capital in service competition and trade,[2] they have not taken the next logical step, which is to analyse the competitive strength among trading nations' varying systems of schooling, training, and learning. Since free trade in a number of professional services will ultimately require a mutual recognition of school certificates and university degrees, we expect this topic to be fully explored in the not too distant future.

Fruitful Avenues for Future Research

During this study, we encountered a number of important service sector industrial organization issues which appear to have remained relatively unexplored. First is the question of the conceptual and empirical evidence and inter-industry variability of economies of scale and economies of scope. Whether services can and will be provided as highly standardized or highly differentiated products (e.g., discount broker versus full service broker) has rather important implications for industrial concentration, entry behaviour, and trade. Preliminary data on annual pay of workers seem to suggest large intra-industry differences in productivity. More research on product type, productivity, and economies of scale is needed to shed light on the expected competitive behaviour of the service sector. A second question which deserves further attention concerns the causes underlying the uneven distribution of technology among service sector organizations and industries. Finally, there remain a number of open questions regarding the varied determinants of part-time employment and pay. In particular, it would be useful to gather industry cross-sectional and in-depth case study evidence on the conditions surrounding part-time employment, productivity, and remuneration of female labour.

NOTES

1. For a good discussion of this point see *Labour Market Flexibility: The Current Debate*, OECD, 1986.

2. See James Melvin's address to the service sector meeting in Ottawa, *Policy Conclusions Arising from the Volume Trade in Services: A Theoretical Analysis*, Ottawa, 1988.

BIBLIOGRAPHY

Abernathy, W.J., K.B. Clark and A.M. Kantrow (1983) *Industrial Rennaissance*, New York, Basic Books.

Ackoff, Russell L., Paul Broholm and Roberta Snow (1984) *Revitalizing Western Economies*, San Francisco, Jersey Bass Publications.

Agarwal, N.C. (1982) "Male-Female Pay Inequity and Public Policy in Canada and the U.S.," *Relations Industrielles*, vol. 37, no. 4, pp. 780-804.

Andersson, Mats, Bruszt Gabor, Eric Hafström and Jonsson Anders (1987) *Changes in Work Patterns and Their Educational Implications*, The Swedish Report to the OECD, Stockholm, M-Gruppen.

Bacon, R. and W. Eltis (1976) *Britain's Economic Problem: Too Few Producers*, London, Macmillan.

Bailey, M.N. (1981) "Productivity and the Services of Capital and Labor," *Brookings Papers on Economic Activity*, vol. 2.

Bailey, M.N. (1982) "The Productivity Growth Slowdown by Industry," *Brookings Papers on Economic Activity*, vol. 2, no. 1.

Baumol, W. (1982) Productivity and the Shift to Services (mimeo).

Baumol, William and Edward N. Wolff (1983) "Feedback from Productivity Growth to R & D," *Scandinavian Journal of Economics*, 85, pp. 147-57.

Baumol, William J. (1985) "Productivity Policy and the Service Sector," in Inman, R. (ed.) *Managing the Service Economy: Prospects and Problems*, Cambridge, Cambridge University Press.

Beckermann, W. (1979) *Slow Growth in Britain*, Oxford, Clarendon Press.

Belcourt, M. and Klaus Weiermair (1988) "Promoting Women Entrepreneurship," *Journal of Economic Planning* (in press).

Benimadhu, Prem (1986) "Labour Resists Tide Toward Part-Time Work," *Canadian Business Review Summer*, pp. 21-23.

Betcherman, Gordon (1982) *Meeting Skill Requirements: Report of the Human Resources Survey Economic Council of Canada*, Ottawa, Supply and Services Canada.

Berger S. and M.J. Piore (1980) *Dualism and Discontinuity in Industrial Societies*, Cambridge: Cambridge University Press.

Birch, David L. (1979) *The Job Creation Process*, Cambridge, Mass., MIT Program on Neighbourhood and Regional Change.

Bluestone, B. and B. Harrison (1982) *The Deindustrialization of America*, New York, Basic Books.

Bobbit R. and J. Ford (1980) "Decision Maker Choice as a Determinant of Organisational Structure," *Academy of Management Review*, pp. 13-23.

Bonamy, Joël (1986) *Les Services informatiques, Evolution du Marche du Travail et Besoins de Formation*, Research Report for OECD/CERI, Lyon, CEDES-CNRS-ECONOMIE ET HUMANISME.

Boyd, Monica and E. Humphreys (1979) *Labour Markets and Sex Differences in Canadian Incomes, Economic Council of Canada*, Discussion Paper No. 143.

Brekenridge, J. (1985) "Equal Pay's Unequal Effects," *Report on Business Management*, vol. 2, no. 6.

Browning, H.C. and J. Singelmann (1978) "The Transformation of the U.S. Labor Force: The Interaction of Industry and Occupation," *Politics and Society*, 8 (7-4), pp. 481-509.

Bruno, M. and J. Sachs (1982) "Input Price Shocks and the Slowdown in Economic Growth: Estimates for U.K. Manufacturing," *Review of Economic Studies*, vol. 49.

Campbell, J.G. (1983) "Equal Pay for Work of Equal Value in the Federal Public Service of Canada," *Compensation Review*, vol. 15, no. 3, pp. 42-52.

Channon, D.F. (1978) *The Service Industries*, London, Macmillan.

Chase, R. (1978) "Where Does the Customer Fit in a Service Operation," *Harvard Business Review*, 56, no. 6, pp. 137-142.

Cornwall, J. (1977) *Modern Capitalism, Its Growth and Transformation*, Oxford, Martin Robertson.

de Bandt, Jacques (1985) (ed.) *Les services dans les societes industrielles avancees*, Paris, Economica.

Denison, E. (1973) "The Shift to Services and the Rate of Productivity Change," *Survey of Current Business*, 53, 10, (Oct.) pp. 20-35.

Department of Regional Industrial Expansion (1985) IA Study of Job Creation in Canada 1974-1982, Ottawa, DRIE.

Diewert, W.E. (1974) "The Effects of Unionization on Wages and Employ-ment: A General Equilibrium Analysis," *Economic Inquiry*, 12, pp. 319-339.

Duchesne, Doreen (1985) *Multiple Job Holders by Industry and Occupa-tion*, Statistics Canada, Labour Force Activity Section, Ottawa, Mini-stry of Supply and Services.

Dumas, Cecile (1986) "Occupational Trends Among Women in Canada: 1976-1985," Statistics Canada, Feature article in *The Labour Force*, catalogue 71-001.

Dunning, John (1987) "The Eclectic Paradigm of International Production: A Restatement and Some Possible Extensions," *Journal of Interna-tional Business Studies* (forthcoming).

Eberts, Mary (1979) "Enforcing Equal Pay and Equal Opportunity Legisla-tion: Mission Impossible," in *Issues and Options: Equal Pay/Equal Opportunity*, Toronto, Ministry of Labour.

Economic Council of Canada (1982) *In Short Supply: Jobs and Skills in the 1980s*, Ottawa, Minister of Supply and Services.

Economic Council of Canada (1985) *Proceedings of a Colloquium on the Economic Status of Women in the Labour Market*, Ottawa, Ministry of Supply and Services.

Economic Council of Canada (1987) *Innovation and Jobs in Canada*, Ot-tawa, Minister of Supply and Services.

Employment and Immigration Canada (1977) *Interdepartmental Evalua-tion Study of the Canada Manpower Training Program*, Technical Report, Ottawa, Employment and Immigration Program Evaluation Branch.

Employment and Immigration Canada (1981) *Labor Market Development in the 1980s*, Ottawa, Ministry of Supply and Services.

European Foundation for the Improvement of Living and Working Condi-tions (1985) *The Role of the Parties Involved in the Introduction of New Technology*, Dublin, European Foundation.

Faulhaber, Gerald, Eli Noam and Roberta Tasley (eds.) (1986) *Services in Transition: The Impact of Information Technology on the Service Sec-tor*, Cambridge, Mass., Ballinger.

Fossum, E. (1983) *Computerisation of Working Life*, Chichester, E. Hor-wood Publishers.

Fuchs, Victor (1982) *Economic Growth and the Rise of Service Employment*, Report No. 257, New York, National Bureau of Economic Research.

Fuchs, Victor R. (1968) *The Service Economy*, New York, National Bureau of Economic Research.

Gershuny, J.I. and I.D. Miles (1983) *The New Service Economy: the transformation of employment in industrial societies*, London, F. Pinter.

Ginsberg, A. (1982) *Good Jobs, Bad Jobs, No Jobs*, Cambridge, Mass., Harvard University Press.

Grubel, Herbert and Michael Walker (1987) *A Theory of Service Sector Growth*, The Fraser Institute, Service Project Discussion Paper 87-6.

Gunderson, Morley (1978) "The Influence of the Status and Sex Composition of Occupations on the Male-Female Earnings Gap," *Industrial and Labour Relations Review*, XXXI, January, pp. 217-226.

Gunderson, Morley (1979) "Decomposition of Male-Female Earnings Differentials Canada 1970," *Canadian Journal of Economics*, August, pp. 479-485.

Hill, P.T. (1977) "On Goods and Services," *Review of Income and Wealth*, December (1).

Hirschhorn, Larry (1987) *Skill Formation in the Service Economy: Final Report of the Work of the American Team for the OECD*, Pittsburgh, Wharton Center for Applied Research, University of Pennsylvania.

Holmstrom, Bengt (1985) "The Provision of Service in a Market Economy," in Inman, R. (ed.), *Managing the Service Economy— Prospects and Problems*, Cambridge, Mass., Cambridge University Press.

Industrial Relations Centre Queen's University (1987) *The Current Industrial Relations Scene in Canada*, Kingston, Queen's University.

Ianrif (1984) *Informatisation et emploi: un bilan des etudes et recherches financees a l'administration*, La documentation francaise.

ILO (1973) *Part-Time Employment: An International Survey*, Geneva, ILO.

Inman, Robert P. (ed.) (1985) *Managing the Service Economy—Prospects and Problems*, Cambridge, Mass., Cambridge University Press.

Jain, H.C. (1982) "Canadian Legal Approaches to Sex Equality in the Workplace," *Monthly Labour Review*, vol. 105, no. 10, pp. 38-42, October.

Kaldor, N. (1966) *Causes of the Slow Rate of Growth in the United Kingdom,* Cambridge, Cambridge University Press.

Knight, Thomas R. (1985) *Recent Trends in Collective Bargaining Over Technological Change,* Proceedings of the 23rd Annual Meeting of the Canadian Industrial Relations Association, pp. 418-429.

Kosters, Marvin (1966) "Income and Substitution Effects in a Family Supply Model," *Reprint Monographs,* Santa Monica, The Rand Corporation, p. 3339.

Krineser, J. Thomas (1976) "The Full-Time Work Week in the United States 1900-1970," *Industrial and Labor Relations Review,* 30, no. 1, pp. 3-15.

Kumar, P. and T. Stengos (1985) "Measuring the Union Relative Wage Impact: A Methodological Note," *Canadian Journal of Economics,* vol. 18, no. 1, February.

Kuttner, Bob (1983) "The Declining Middle," *The Atlantic Monthly,* July, pp. 60-72.

Labour Canada (1982) *In the Chips: Opportunities, People, Partnerships,* Ottawa, Supply and Services Canada.

Labour Canada (1983) *Part-Time Work in Canada,* Ottawa, Supply and Services Canada.

Lawrence, R.Z. (1984) *Can America Compete?,* Washington, D.C., The Brookings Institution.

Leach, Donald and Howard Wagstaff (1986) *Future Employment and Technological Change,* London, Kogan Page.

Leibenstein, Harvey (1966) "Allocative Efficiency vs. 'X-efficiency'," *American Economic Review,* vol 56, no. 3, 392-415.

Leslie, Peter M. (1980) *Canadian Universities 1980 and Beyond; Enrollment, Structural Change and Finance,* Policy Study No. 3, Ottawa, Association of Universities and Colleges of Canada.

Lewis G. Harold (1963) *Unionism and Relative Wages in the United States,* Chicago, University of Chicago Press.

Lewis, W.A. (1978) *Growth and Fluctuations 1870-1913,* London, Allen & Unwin.

Lingh, A. (1977) "U.K. Industry and the World Economy: A Case of Deindustrialization," *Cambridge Journal of Economics.*

Little, T.D. (1986) "Part-Time Work: Crisis or Opportunity," *Canadian Business Review*, Spring, pp. 18-20.

Lowe, Graham S. (1981) "Causes of Unionization in Canadian Banks," *Relations Industrielles*, vol. 36, no. 7, pp. 865-892.

Maddison, A. (1982) *Phases of Capitalist Development*, Oxford, Oxford University Press.

Macdonald, Glen (1983) "The Size and Structure of Union-Non-Union Wage Differentials in Canadian Industry," *Canadian Journal of Economics*, 16, pp. 480-485.

Magun, Sunder (1982) "The Rise of Service Employment in the Canadian Economy," *Relations Industrielles*, vol. 37, no. 3, pp. 528-559.

Magun, Sunder (1985) "The Effects of Technological Change on the Labour Market in Canada," *Relations Industrielles*, vol. 40, no. 4, pp. 720-743.

Maki, Dennis R. (1978) "An Evaluation of Canadian Federal Manpower Policies: Training and Job Creation," (mimeo) Background Study for the Economic Council of Canada.

Marquand, Judith (1979) "The Service Sector and Regional Policy in the United Kingdom," Research Series 29, Centre for Environmental Studies, London, England.

McGrath, Paul (1984) "Timothy Would be Shocked," *Canadian Business*, August, pp. 58-60.

Menzies, Heather (1981) *Women and the Chip*, Montreal, Institute for Research on Public Policy.

Mills, Peter K. (1986) *Managing Service Industries: Organisational Practices in a Postindustrial Economy*, Cambridge, Mass., Ballinger.

Mills, Peter and N. Marqulies (1980) "Toward a Core Typology of Service Organisations," *Academy of Management Review*, 5, pp. 255-265.

Nakamura, Alice and Masao Nakamura (1985) *The Second Paycheck: A Socioeconomic Analysis of Earnings*, Orlando, Academic Press.

Nordhaus, W.D. (1982) "Economic Policy and Declining Productivity Growth," *European Economic Review*, 18, pp. 131-57.

OECD (1985) *Employment Growth and Structural Change*, Paris, OECD.

OECD (1986) *Flexibility in the Labour Market: The Current Debate*, Paris, OECD.

OECD/CERI (1986) "The Evolution of New Technology, Work and Skills in the Service Sector," (mimeo) Paris, OECD/CERI.

Ontario Manpower Commission (1986) *Training in Industry: A Survey of Employer-Sponsored Programs in Ontario*, Toronto, Ontario Manpower Commission.

Ontario Ministry of Treasury and Economics (1986), *Ontario Study of the Service Sector*, Queen's Printer, Toronto.

Ontario Study of the Service Sector, Background Papers (1986) Government of Ontario, Ministry of Treasury and Economics.

Ontario Task Force on Employment and New Technology (1985) *Employment and New Technology in Ontario's Service Sector: A Summary of Selected Industries*, Toronto, Queen's Printer.

Ontario Task Force on Hours of Work and Overtime (1987) *Working Times: The Report of the Ontario Task Force on Hours of Work and Overtime*, Toronto, Ontario Ministry of Labour.

Peitchinis, S. (1984) "Employment in the Evolving Information Economy," Royal Society of Canada. Conference on the Information Economy, Toronto.

Petit, Pascal (1986) *Slow Growth and the Service Economy*, London, Frances Pinter.

Picot, Garnett W. (1986) *Canada's Industries: Growth in Jobs Over Three Decades*, Statistics Canada, Social and Economic Studies Division, Ottawa, Ministry of Supply and Services.

Porat, M. (1977) *The Information Economy, Definitions and Measurement*, Washington: U.S. Department of Commerce.

Postner, Harry & Lesle M. Wesa (1987) *Sources of Canadian Employment Change: A Decomposition Analysis*, Discussion Paper No. 339, Ottawa, Economic Council of Canada.

Posyniak, Len (1986) "Let's Take a Fresh Look at Alternative Work Time," *Canadian Business*, September, pp. 76-115.

Public Service Alliance of Canada (1982) "Technological Change," *The Review*, June, pp. 11-17.

Rajam, Amin (1987) *Services—The Second Industrial Revolution?*, London, Institute of Manpower Studies.

Reid, Frank (1983) *Protecting Part-Time Workers: Defining the Scope of the Problem*, Toronto, Centre for Industrial Relations.

Reid, F. and G. Swartz (1982) *Prorating Fringe Benefits for Part-Time Employees in Canada,* Toronto, Centre for Industrial Relations.

Riddell, Craig (1986) *Adapting to Change: Labour Market Adjustment in Canada,* vol. 18, Royal Commission on the Economic Union and Development Prospects for Canada, Toronto, University of Toronto Press.

Riddle, Dorothy I. (1986) *Service-Led Growth: The Role of the Service Sector in World Development,* New York, Praeger Special Studies.

Robb, R.E. (1984) "Equal Pay Policy," *Toward Equity: Proceedings of a Colloquium on the Economic Status of Women in the Labour Market,* November, Ottawa, Economic Council of Canada.

Rothwell, Ray and Walter Zegveld (1979) *Technical Change and Employment,* New York, St. Martin's Press.

Sabolo, Yves (1975) *The Service Industries,* Geneva, ILO.

Sautter, C. (1979) "L'adaption du Japon au ralentissement de la croissance et à la ponction exterieure," *Revue Economique,* 30, 6, November.

Scholz, A. and A. Lippe (1987) *Changes in Work Patterns and Their Educational Impact—Adjustments in Work Organization,* Training and Technology in the Service Sector in West Germany, Research report submitted to OECD/CERI, Göttingen, SOFI.

Schultze, Ch. L. (1983) "Industrial Policy: A Dissent," *The Brookings Review,* p. 3.

Shelp, Ronald, K. (1979) *Beyond Industrialization: Ascendancy of the Global Service Economy, New York, Praeger.*

Skolker, J.V. (1976) "Long Term Effects of Unbalanced Labour Productivity Growth: On the Way to a Self-Service Society," in J. Szalai, N. de Pasouier (eds.) *Private and Enlarged Consumption,* Amsterdam, North Holland.

Stanback, T., P. Bearse, T. Noyelle and R. Kapasek (1981) *Services: The New Economy,* Totowa, N.J., Allanheld, Osmun & Co..

Statistic Canada (1973) *Training in Industry 1969-70,* catalogue 81-555, Ottawa, Ministry of Supply and Services.

Statistics Canada (1978) *Employee Compensation in Canada. All Industries,* catalogue 72-618. Ottawa, Ministry of Supply and Services.

Statistics Canada (1981) *Job Market Reality for Post-Secondary Students,* Ottawa, Ministry of Supply and Services.

Statistics Canada (1985) *Self-Employment in Canada,* catalogue 71-582, Ottawa, Ministry of Supply and Services.

Statistics Canada (1985b) *Multiple Job Holders by Industry and Occupation,* catalogue 71-X-512, Ottawa, Ministry of Supply and Services.

Statistics Canada (1981) *Part-Time Employment in 1975 and 1976,* by M. Webber, Labour Force Survey Division, Research Section, Ottawa, Supply and Services.

Statistics Canada (1986) *Employment Creation in Canada: A Longitudinal Assessment of Industry, Firm Size and Country of Control 1978-1982,* Ministry of Supply and Services, Ottawa, catalogue 18-501.

Stigler, G.J. (1956) *Trends in Employment in the Service Industries,* Princeton: Princeton University Press.

Thomas, D.R.E. (1975) "Strategy is Different in Service Business," *Harvard Business Review,* 56 (4) pp. 158-65.

Tolbert C., P.M. Moram and E.M. Beck (1980) "The Structure of Economic Segmentation: A Dual Economy Approach," *American Journal of Sociology,* 85 (3) pp. 1095-1116.

Urquhart, M. (1981) "Are Services Recession-Proof?," *Monthly Labor Review.*

Urquhart, M. (1984) "The Employment Shift to Services—Where Did it Come From?," *Monthly Labor Review,* no. 107, 4, pp. 15-22.

U.S. Department of Commerce (1976) *U.S. Service Industries in World Markets and Current Problems and Future Policy Developments,* Washington: U.S. Department of Commerce.

Verdoorn, P.J. (1949) "Fattori che regolano lo sviluppo della produttività del lavoro," *L'industria,* pp. 3-10.

Weisskopf, T., J. Bowles and D. Gordon (1983) "Hearts and Minds: A Social Model of U.S. Productivity Growth," *Brookings Papers on Economic Activity,* vol. 2.

Weiermair, Klaus (1984) *Apprenticeship Training in Canada: A Theoretical and Empirical Analysis Economic Council of Canada,* Discussion Paper No. 250.

Weiermair, Klaus (1986) "Secular Changes in Youth Labour Markets and Youth Unemployment in Canada," *Relations Industrielles,* vol. 41, no. 3, pp. 469-490.

Weiermair, Klaus (1987) "Part-Time Labour: Causes and Consequences for Managerial Discretion," in Dlugos and Weiermair (eds.) *Management Under Differing Employment Systems and Labor Market Conditions*, Berlin, de Gryter (in press).

Wong, G.G., C.A. Schultz and G.A. Growe (1985) "Evaluation of the Entrepreneurial Immigration Program," prepared for Employment and Immigragtion Canada, Program Evaluation Branch.

DATE DUE

DEC 8 1993			